A PRACTICAL GUIDE

Raspberry Pi PBX

FOR AN ALMOST WIRELESS VOIP TELEPHONE SYSTEM

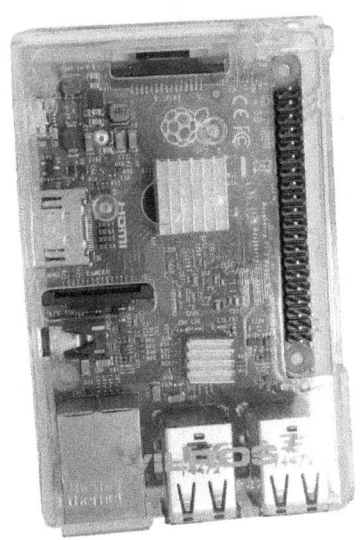

Joe Yeung
December 2016

Copyright © 2016 by Joe Yeung. All right reserved.

All product names and services identified throughout this book are trademarks or registered trademarks of respective companies. They are used throughout this book only for the benefit of those companies. No such uses or the use of any trade name is conveying endorsement or other affiliation with the book. The domain project.org.uk is used for illustration purposes for this book only. It is used to describe the organisation as a project; it is not intended to be associated with the actual owners of the domain.

Notice of Rights
All rights reserved. No part of this book may be reproduced or transmitted in any form by any means, electronic, mechanical, photocopying, recording, or otherwise, without the prior written permission of the publisher.

Notice of Liability
The information in this book is distributed on an "As Is" basis, without warranty. While every precaution has been taken in the preparation of this book, neither the author nor the publisher, shall have any liability to any person or entity with respect to any loss or damage caused or alleged to be cause directly or indirectly by the instructions contained in this book or by the software, hardware products or services described in it.

References:-
Nerd Vittles - The Sensational Raspberry Pi 3 Featuring Incredible PBX™ GUI with Raspbian 8 Jessie http://nerdvittles.com/?p=17094

ISBN 978-1-326-89814-4

Contents

Introduction 4

The scenario 6

A Raspberry Pi? Really? 10

Alternatives? 14

Setting up the "Pi" 40

Setting up the PBX 49

Telephone System requirements 56

Configuring the PBX 59

Interactive Voice Response 78

Conclusion 96

Some commonly used terms 97

Introduction

The Raspberry Pi

It was developed and built as a low-cost board to help encourage the understanding, learning and continued study of computing in schools. Besides being an educational tool, it can be used for a wide range of tasks, very often, these tasks are business applications performed by standard desktop computers e.g. like spreadsheets, word processing and internet browsing can effectively run from a Raspberry Pi.

Because it comes only as a circuit board with a various input and output connectors, it normally requires at least a case (to protect it from physical damage), a monitor, a keyboard and a mouse to operate.

Due to its small size, and it is not a lot bigger than a credit card, it is particularly useful for use as an embedded device. One example is using it as an embedded controller for home appliances controllable by a smart phone.

The "Pi" has been used for many fun projects like creating a media stream player, a wireless audio system controller and a smart beer fridge etc. But on this occasion, I am going to use it as a serious business tool. I will use the "Pi" as a PBX for an almost wireless telephone system for a charity project that requires a business class telephone system.

In my book "VOIP - a practical guide for the non-telephone engineer", I described the design and implementation of a real-life low cost business telephone system that can be carried out by anyone with reasonable ICT knowledge. In this book, I will do the same, except the budget and the circumstances are completely different. Although in this case, the project is completely fictitious, the aims of both the books are the same - a low cost business class telephone system that is designed to be used as a business tool in a real life.

Whilst it would be very tempting to just jump into what to get and how to configure the system, this book is not about a fun project. It is about using a low cost device as a proper business tool. The business case must be proven first and it must present a better solution than any other system that is available. Costs and benefits must be shown and it must run reliably and ultimately, satisfies the business needs of the project that will depend on it.

This book sets out to solve a business situation where a temporary project office requires an effective and feature rich telephone system comparable to that of conventional telephone systems. The situation presented makes a conventional telephone system not viable within the budget constraints of the project.

This book demonstrates that by using some innovative thinking and utilising technical knowledge and skills, an extremely low cost telephone system can be implemented to benefit organisations on the tightest of budgets. And the main player for this project is a Raspberry Pi (used by lots of schools for education purposes)! Who would have thought that a Raspberry Pi can be used as the basic building block of a telephone system? And yet, in the next few chapters, I will show you how it can be done.

The project is based on two separate modules, both requiring minimal, or no data cabling, to achieve wireless communication. They are:

- Mobile technology for internet access, voice calls and SMS
- DECT technology to create local telephone extensions

The main reason for considering an almost pure wireless technology is due to the specific circumstances that the project finds itself in. As a project that is potentially only going to run for 6 months and with very limited funding.

The project is faced with having to operate in 3 different rooms with no direct telephone connection with each other. Connecting the rooms together via cabling would be very costly, so the only alternative is to use wireless technology. Fortunately, with the general availability of 4G internet service within most cities, this type of system can work effectively and the costs are surprisingly low too.

The scenario

A social enterprise project to help young people find jobs has just received funding approval to run for 6 months with the potential of extension pending on how successful the project is. The project has the following objectives:-

- a drop-in centre for employment advice
- CV writing assistance
- basic office skills training
- internet job search
- arranging job interviews for young people

The project requires a base within the funding area in the city and must have all the necessary equipment like computers with internet access for emails and job searches etc., a printer, fax capabilities and a telephone system. A large 40 square metre room was potentially available on easy in easy out terms provided by another charity project that runs multiple small workshop units. There are several other smaller units vacant most of the time, so finding a base for the project within this workshop should not present any problems.

Now, let us make this proposal a little more challenging by putting in an obstacle to our project. The situation is realistic and can well be faced by small organisations in real life. When the project proposal was written, the costing of a telephone system was not properly evaluated. The assumption was that a telephone system with 2 lines (BT Versatility with basic transfer function for 4 telephones), which was already installed in the room, was available for £500. However, from the time the project was perceived and the approval given, circumstances have changed and the large office available then is no longer available. Although three small units are still available, they are independent rooms separated by other rooms and are about 10 metres from each other, to make it worst, one room is on the next floor up. So the original plan of having an existing telephone system for the project is no longer valid.

The project was referred back to the original ICT advisor and he made the following suggestions:-

- all computers will be linked by WIFI
- one telephone line (BT feature line) to be installed in every room

For the computers, WIFI links should be fine, however, the cost of 3 feature lines (including installation cost) would be an order of magnitude higher and it was not budgeted. Any extra expenditure will have to come from savings from somewhere else which is going to problematic. Since the length of the project could be as short as 6 months, commitment to lengthy contracts would be very difficult. The original plan for 2 lines with a minimum of 12 months contract already means that the project will have to pay the whole 12 months whether it gets extra funding to continue or not.

The management committee is now faced with the decision of whether to look for premises somewhere else or to scrap the project altogether. It is extremely difficult to find premises to rent for such a short period of time and to give up the project after all the months of hard work and negotiations would be a massive disappointment for those involved. It will also be letting down all those who would have benefited from the services provided by the project. The committee must find a solution of the telephone system situation as soon as possible.

Several meetings with the ICT advisor have yielded no further progress. The biggest stumbling block has been that the project is potentially only going to run for 6 months, no commitment can be made for longer and hence cheaper deals. Several suggestions have been made including:-

- using only one telephone and everyone shares the telephone
- using 3 telephone lines, one in each room
- using mobile phones one in each room

The picture below shows how the rooms are separated:-

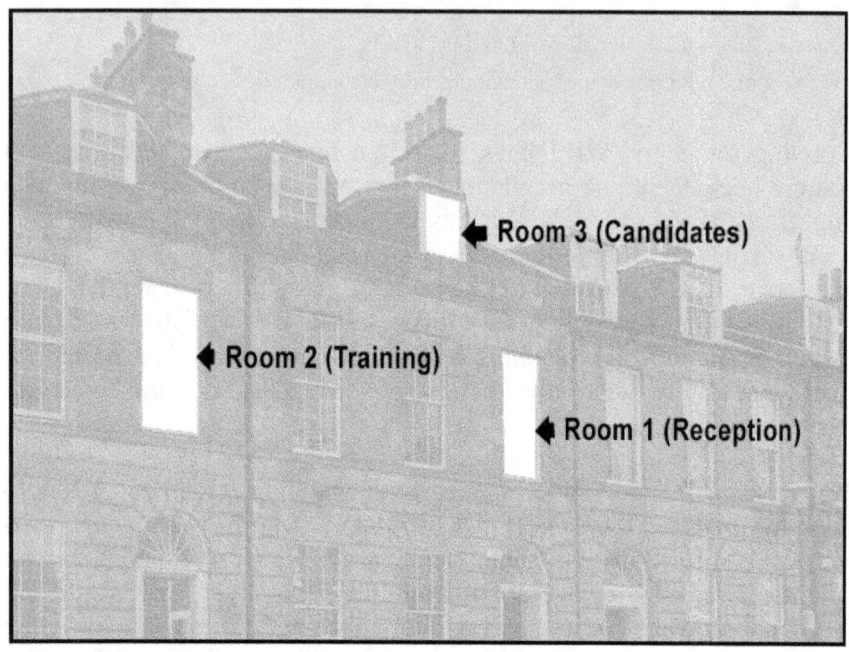

The proposal of having only one telephone for the project will satisfy the cost criteria, however, it will mean the inconvenience of half a dozen people in different rooms sharing only one telephone. This idea was rejected as totally unrealistic. By installing a single telephone line to each room, the cost would still have been too high and transfer of calls between rooms would not have been possible. Mobile phones for each room were closest to being accepted, but eventually rejected due to the inability to transfer calls between rooms. After all, a mobile phone number for the project does not present a very professional image to the public. In particular, applying for funding from other charities would not fill the potential funders with confidence about their proposal.

The project was in danger of having to be delayed or even cancelled when the grandson of one of the committee members mentioned about his school project in which a Raspberry Pi was used as a PBX for a telephone system. He was told that a Raspberry Pi only cost £50 and the telephone system can do a lot of things that would cost hundreds if not thousands of pounds.

An urgent plea was made by the committee member's grandson to the teacher who is responsible for the Raspberry Pi project to see if he can help.

Mr. George Johnstone, the teacher who runs the school Raspberry Pi PBX project, is initially surprised that he is approached. After giving the project some serious thoughts, he has decided that he is able to help. With a strong background in information technology and experience in IP telephony, setting up a telephone system represents an interesting challenge to him.

After successfully setting up the Raspberry Pi PBX project for the school, he is convinced that the idea is good, and will definitely work reliably and work well too.

Initial perception of a workable telephone system using 4G /Raspberry Pi / DEC phones as shown below:-

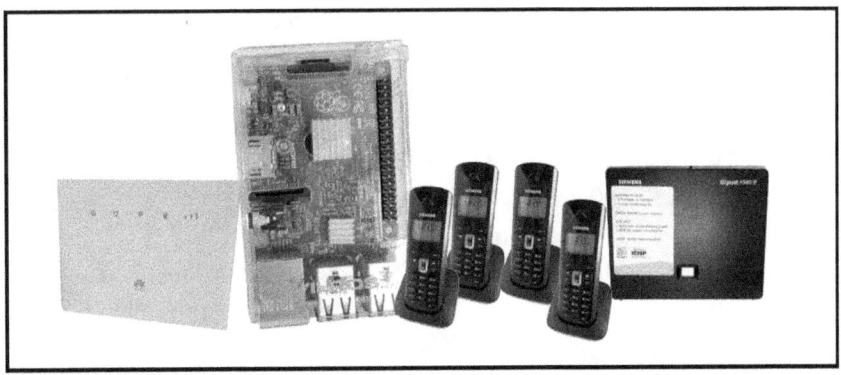

A Raspberry Pi? Really?

George is confident about the reliability and capability of the Raspberry Pi and proceeds with developing a proposal for the committee to consider. When the potential of using a Raspberry Pi is mentioned, most of the committee laughed and thought it was a joke. It is now up to George to convince everyone that the system is viable, cost effective and will work well for the project.

Telephone lines or not

The first consideration is what type of lines can be used for the telephone calls. Obviously, the first consideration is to use a PSTN line or two which was envisaged at the beginning. Using British Telecom prices and packages (published on their website as guides, the following information on potential costs can be estimated.

In general, these packages have fixed length contracts, meaning penalty charges if the contracts are terminated early. In addition, there are installation charges /activation charges which may add up to hundreds of pounds. On the other hand, unlimited calls to landlines and mobiles can be added to the packages at £9 per month per line. Furthermore, by using the BT broadband package, the installation / activation fees can be waived. The available packages are as follows:-

Value phone line (24months contract)

- From £15.90 /month + installation charge
- Includes 2 phone features
- Online exclusive offer - unlimited calls to UK landlines & mobiles for £9 a month
- Online exclusive offer – 2500 minutes to most non-mobile international numbers for £9 a month
- Cannot connect to a phone system

Standard phone line (24 months contract)
- From £21.20 /month + installation charge
- Includes 2 phone features
- Online exclusive offer - unlimited calls to UK landlines & mobiles for £9 a month
- Online exclusive offer – 2500 minutes to most non-mobile international numbers for £9 a month
- Can connect to a phone system

Featureline (60 months contract)
- From £22.40 /month + installation charge
- Includes 14 phone features
- Online exclusive offer - unlimited calls to UK landlines & mobiles for £9 a month
- Online exclusive offer – 2500 minutes to most non-mobile international numbers for £9 a month
- Can connect to a phone system

The first package "Value phone line" can be eliminated as it cannot be linked to a telephone system. So only the "Standard phone line" or the "Featureline" packages can be considered. Since the "Featureline" package is a 60 months contract, early termination would incur serious costs. So the only choice has to be the "Standard phone line".

On the surface of it, the cost of the "Standard phone line" package seems reasonable if the project uses the BT broadband package as well. However, if the project does not receive any funding to continue, then the cost of termination of these services must be taken into account. The committee has admitted to George that the initial planning of the project did not take into consideration the termination charges; they assume that funding will be available. George points out that since funding cannot be guaranteed, the budgeting of these charges must be taken into consideration. The committee agrees, and immediately proceeds to work out the estimated termination charges.

The following section show the early termination charges as displayed on the BT website:-

What are early termination (hold to term) charges?
When you order services from BT there will normally be a minimum contract period of 12, 18 or 24 months. If you decide to stop receiving a service within this minimum contract period, you'll normally have to pay an early termination charge.

What will I be charged?
What you're charged depends on how long is left to run on your minimum contract period. The tables below show how much you're charged for each month remaining. So for example, if you have six months left on your telephone service Unlimited Weekend Calls minimum contract period, you'll have to pay a charge of £7.50 multiplied by six, which is £45.00. You may also have to pay a charge for any equipment we have provided at a reduced cost for use with the service you are ending – see our terms and conditions or Tariff Guide for more details.

Telephone Service	Monthly Charge
Line Rental Only	£7.50
Unlimited Weekend Calls	£7.50
Unlimited Evening & Weekend Calls	£9.25
Unlimited Anytime Calls	£12.50
Home Phone Saver 2019	£9.50
Home Phone Saver 2018	£8.50
Unlimited Weekend Plan	£8.00
Unlimited Evening & Weekend Plan	£9.75
Unlimited Anytime Plan	£11.50
Home Phone Saver 2017	£7.75
Unlimited Anytime Plan Plus	£14.50
Unlimited Anytime Mobile Plan	£6.75

Assuming that the project takes on 2 lines, unlimited anytime calls, the likely cost will be 2 X £12.50 X 6 months = £150. There will also be an early termination charge for the broadband subscription too. The charges are displayed on the BT website as follows:-

BT Total Broadband	Monthly Charge
Option 1	£17.50
Option 2	£22.25
Option 3	£25.00
Faster Total Broadband Option 3	£16.00

The termination charges for broadband based on the table above will be £17.50 X 6 = £105.

Although the costs are displayed very clearly on the BT website, it is difficult to know the actual cost because there are special offers and deals that can be had at different times. So the estimated costs and charges can only be used for budgeting purposes. The total budget (for 6 months) for the telephone and broadband services can be calculated as follows:

- line rental - 2 X £22 X 6 = £264
- call packages - 2 X £9 X 6 = £108
- broadband - 1 x £10 X6 = £60
- early cancellation fees - £150 + £105 = £255

The approximate total cost for the telephone and internet usage for 6 months will be £687. The original projection for the telephone system /broadband of £1000 is not too far out. By shopping around, it is assumed that better deals can be had, but the ball park figure will not be significantly different. The issue now is that there is no current system to utilise the telephone lines and the telephone system has to reach 3 different rooms on 2 separately floors.

Alternatives?

Now that George has established the cost of one alternative, he is now able to look for other alternatives that may be better in terms of costs and service. The most obvious choice is to utilise the internet for all telephone calls, commonly called internet telephony. Internet telephony is frequently confused with VOIP (Voice over Internet Protocol). Although VOIP can be used by internet telephony for voice calls, a VOIP telephone system does not require a connection to the internet to operate.

Internet telephony

It is possible to use the internet for all the telecommunications without the need of a PBX by using a hosted service. Typically, this service provides the equivalent of a local PBX and incurs very low initial investments. All that is normally required is a monthly subscription plus the purchase of the number of SIP telephones required.

One local provider which has been used by George is Soho66. This SIP provider offers a multi user line/call package together with a local telephone number for Newcastle. The advertised price for unlimited calls to local and national numbers for up to 5 users including a local number for £13.00 + VAT. This means that for the same price or less than a standard telephone line, the project can have up to 5 lines and no long term commitment. And of course, there are many other SIP providers on the market to choose from too, so this choice is well worth considering.

As for using normal broadband for making and receiving calls, it depends on various factors which may affect how well it works.

- upstream speed
- contention ratio
- service providers quality of service
- local equipment

Very often, people assume the downstream speed (frequently quoted by internet providers) is the actual speed of the internet connection up and downstream, it is not the case, the upstream speed is normally only about 1Mbit.

Standard broadband connections are also shared by many other users, for businesses, it can be up to 19 other users. These users can equate to even more users as businesses tend to have a network with many users sharing their own connections. This means that at any given time, an internet connection can have up to 20 businesses all downloading and uploading emails, images and files etc. Since a telephone conversation is a 2 way process, both the upstream and downstream speed are important.

There are numerous articles available explaining the bandwidth requirements for a good quality voice conversation. In general, it is accepted that only 100Kbs (Kilobits per second) is required, but in reality, it is recommended that 3Mbs (Megabit per second) is needed for the best results.

For the project, with the potential of some 19 other businesses sharing the same connection, the standard 1Mbit upstream speed may not be enough to allow for consistent clear conversations.

Experience tells him that whilst normal broadband can be used for telephone calls over the internet, it is likely to suffer loss of quality from time to time. The problems tend to manifest as delays, echoes and broken conversations. This tends to happen when the network is busy, so internet telephony over a normal broadband connection is probably not a realistic alternative.

In order to use this service successfully, a really high speed (both upstream and downstream) and reliable internet connection is required. This means a normal internet connection based on standard broadband may not be adequate.

One idea that has crossed his mind is the possibility of using fibre for internet access as well as for telephone calls, unfortunately, after some research; he has discovered that neither BT nor Virgin offer fibre to the premises. So this idea is a non-starter. On any account, even if there is a fibre connection available, in order to use standard SIP phones, the project will need a LAN connection between the three rooms which will mean running cables between them.

Mobile technology

With the availability of 4G internet access all over the city, George thinks there is enough merit to give this alternative serious consideration. He first needs to establish if there is 4G access in the area and if so, is it good and reliable.

He asks the committee members with 4G smart phones to visit the premises at different times of the day and run speed tests to gauge the performance of various mobile operators in that area. The test is carried out over several days and the results of the speed tests are impressive.

The screen grab (speedtest.net by Ookla) below shows the speed of 4G access from the planned project office:-

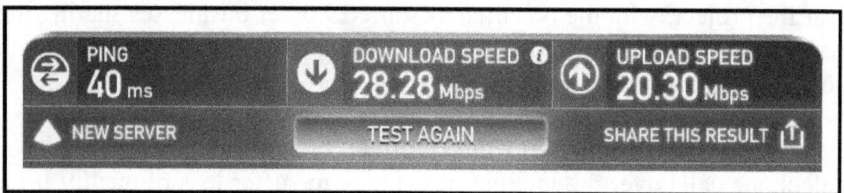

Everyone reports download speeds of between 25Mbit to 35Mbit and upload speeds of between 15Mbit to 25Mbit. The results are not exactly surprising as the workshop is situated within the city centre and less than 400 metres from most mobile providers' masts.

The results are extremely encouraging for George as he knows that, mobile technology is a realistic alternative to normal telephone lines and conventional broadband.

The availability of 4G represents the key to allowing George to develop his proposal as a realistic alternative. In his mind, he already knows that 4G would be the solution. All he needs now is to find a package that is economically viable. The project needs internet access and a business class telephone system. Looking at the packages that are available, all mobile providers provide SIM only deals that can be pay as you go, pay monthly, yearly or longer. In fact, most monthly deals work out more expensive if the project runs for only six months if termination charges are applied. So the project is now going to have to look at 12 month deals. The advantage is that it will cost the project less and should the project be extended, there will not be any termination charges at all.

So what is available?

O2's offer

Screen grab on O2 site showing O2 package with 10GB data and unlimited calls and texts

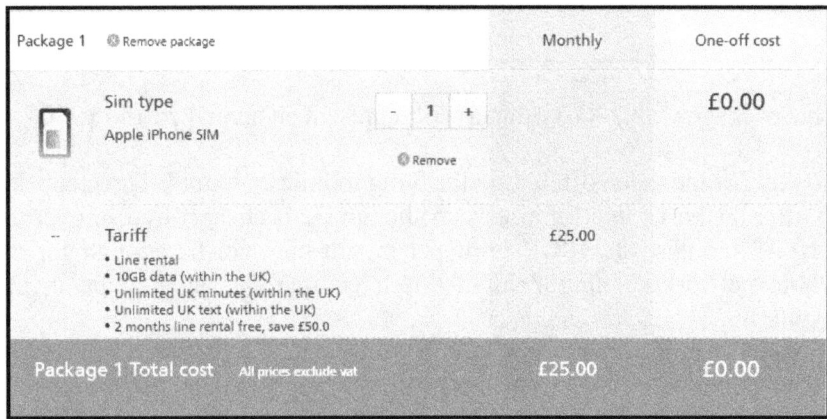

Screen grab above shows O2 package which includes a 2 months line rental free period, reducing the annual cost to £250.

EE's offer

EE PAYM 4G Multi SIM - £34.99 monthly

- Extra Plan - double speed 4G
- Unlimited minutes
- Unlimited text messages
- 16 GB data
- 12 months plan
- This package with 16GB of data will represent an annual cost to nearly £420.

Three's offer

Screen grab below on Three site showing O2 package with 30GB of data and unlimited calls and text:-

30GB data	All-you-can-eat minutes	12 month contract	£30.00 £15.00 a month for 6 months.*	Select plan. See full plan details.

This package with 30GB of data will represent an annual cost to £270

Looking at the value offered by the 3 big mobile operators, Three appears to offer the best value for money. Although O2 is cheaper by £20 over the next 12 months, the 10GB limit per month may not be enough for the whole network of up to half a dozen computers that may be in use regularly.

Some providers like Giffgaff may offer what is called "all-you-can-eat data", but after more detailed research, these packages have a limit for data sharing - also called tethering. The data sharing limit is usually just a few GB, so they are not really good enough for the project.

Based on the speed test results from two committee members who use Three for 4G access, the indication is that their connection speeds were above average most of the time.

Although the proximity to the mobile providers' masts is no guarantee of speed and reliability, nonetheless, it indicates that the location is likely to benefit from better service due to the short distance from them.

As the high speed of the mobile broadband connection can support multiple calls over the internet, it can therefore remove the necessity of multiple telephone lines. The requirement of 2 telephone lines plus a standard broadband package can be replaced by one SIM package.

The following table shows the comparison between the strength and weaknesses of both fixed line and mobile technology to help present the business case.

Fixed line	Mobile
reliability proven	reliability not proven but likely
cost per line + cost of broadband	cost of one SIM package
standard internet speed	very high upstream and downstream speed
unlikely to offer good quality internet calls	likely to offer good quality internet calls
running cost is higher	running cost is lower

The table above shows that if proven reliability is not the main consideration, then mobile technology is the better solution.

So far, 4G mobile technology has been considered only with high speed broadband in mind, can mobile technology do anything else that the project can utilise? Does the mobile package not offer unlimited calls and text as well?

4G WIFI Routers

Just like any standard internet broadband service, 4G also requires a router to allow a network to share an internet connection. The only difference is that the 4G router does not require a physical telephone line or a fibre cable to do so. All it needs a SIM with a relevant data package to operate. If a subscription to a SIP service (internet telephony) is available, users can make normal landline or mobile telephone calls through the provider to any valid destinations.

The search for a 4G WIFI router

To begin with, George searched the World Wide Web for articles on using the Raspberry Pi as a 4G router and preferable a GSM gateway to allow for mobile calls utilising the 4G SIM package. For example, the article called **"How-To: Raspberry Pi as a 3G/4G Router"** link below:-

http://www.g7smy.co.uk/2014/08/raspberry-pi-as-a-3g4g-router/

The link above describes what is needed and how to configure a Raspberry Pi to connect to a ZTE MF823 LTE 4G dongle and make it a 4G router.

What about using the Raspberry Pi as a GSM gateway and allow the mobile calls to be made utilising the SIM package? A very informative article which describes how a Raspberry Pi can be used as a GSM gateway is available on the internet.

Follow the link below:-

http://www.raspberry-asterisk.org/documentation/gsm-voip-gateway-with-chan_dongle/

Local WIFI access

Since the offices are split into three different locations more than 10 metres apart, it is physically not easy to connect them with network cables. The only realistic alternative is WIFI. The following links describes the process of turning a "Pi" into a WIFI hotspot.

https://frillip.com/using-your-raspberry-pi-3-as-a-wifi-access-point-with-hostapd/

All the websites describe in great details on how a Raspberry Pi can be used in conjunction with a compatible 4G USB dongle or a WIFI dongle to act as a 4G router, a WIFI router and a GSM gateway. However, there is no information on how to get the "Pi" to offer all the required functions simultaneously.

Further research reveals that there are lots of compatibility issues. For example, only certain models of certain makes of dongles will work. To make the situation even more confusing, some versions for firmware of even those that work do not work correctly.

After serous considerations, the idea of using the "Pi" as a WIFI router/SMS and GSM gateway is discarded. There is just not the time for trial and error, besides; the project requires a business class system that will run reasonably smoothly and reliably.

4G WIFI router, SMS gateway and GSM gateway all-in-one?

Although it is not immediately possible to use the "Pi" for all the functions required, it still makes good sense to use it as part of the system, the part that the "Pi" is known to work reliably. Due to its low cost, a "Pi" based PBX should still be much cheaper than any PBX appliance on the market. The next step is to see if it is possible to find equipment that will offer the 4G/SMS/GSM functions for a reasonable price.

A quick search on the World Wide Web easily finds lots of 4G routers for less than £100 available in the UK. At the lower cost end, it is possible to get one that requires a 4G dongle to operate. On the opposite end, there are 4G routers with SIM slots that only require activated SIMs with valid data packages. At the very basic level, any good and reliable 4G router should allow for internet sharing plus internet telephony.

What about mobile calls and SMS service?

It is abundantly clear that mobile data only packages are not much less than packages that include unlimited calls and SMS text, so it would make sense to utilising these packages. Of course, it will require a device that can make all the services available to a LAN.

Huawei B315 4G LTE mobile WIFI router

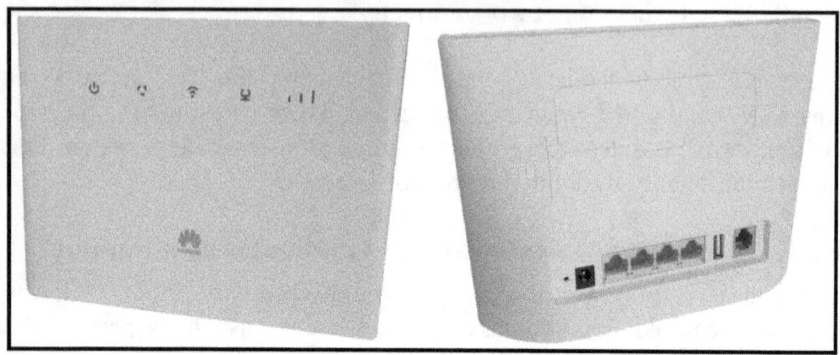

One device stands out as a possibility is the Huawei B315. The product description shows that it is capable of all four functions required, albeit, not quite as straight forward as it seems. It is capable of supporting the following:-

- 4G internet sharing
- WIFI and LAN functions
- SMS service via own web server
- mobile calls via one telephone socket (RJ11)

The price of the device is around £125 and UK stocks are available from local suppliers. However, there is one obvious issue with how to share the telephone socket. It would be very easy to plug a standard telephone to the socket as long as the telephone cable has an RJ11 plug. If not, it is possible to get an adaptor to convert the BT end of the telephone to an RJ11 end to plug into the phone socket of the Router. To use this device and to share this connection with several telephones would be a lot more difficult.

George's school project uses a VOIP to PSTN adaptor (Cisco SPA3102-NA) to connect a normal telephone line to the "Pi". The adaptor has an FXO socket for a connection to a standard telephone line. By connecting this device to the "Pi", it can act as a trunk to be shared by all the SIP phones on the LAN.

Although the Cisco SPA3102 works almost flawlessly in every other respect, landline (PSTN) calls through this device experiences serious echoing. Despite spending a lot of time fine tuning its settings, the problem still persists.

In addition, there is also the problem of connecting telephones from different rooms to the "Pi", after all, there are is no cabling between the different rooms. So the idea of using a VOIP to PSTN adaptor is probably not viable in this case.

The "Pi" has lots of sockets, but no Landline (PSTN) socket to connect to telephone line as below:-

How can several telephones connect to one single PBX without the use of telephone cabling? Once again, a search on the web shows that there is hardly any WIFI SIP phones on the market that are within the price range of the project.

For example the "Unidata INCOMINC ICW-1000G Wi-Fi Phone" cost well over £100 each. 4 of them would have cost nearly £500, and this is in addition to everything else. Besides, it is not possible to use SIP phones like the Incominc Wi-Fi phone to access a standard telephone line without an ATA (Analogue Telephone Adaptor) like the Cisco 3102 anyway. So for the project, it is not really appropriate.

Softphones

A softphone (software telephone) is an application program that enables voice over Internet Protocol (VOIP) telephone calls from computing devices. There are many free/ open-source softphones available e.g. XLite, Qutecom and ZoIPer etc. They can be downloaded from the websites of the vendors as well as many websites dedicated to VOIP.

As softphones are software applications running on computers which can be linked wirelessly to a WIFI router, there will be no need to cabling between rooms for telephone calls.

However, there are several issues:-

- quality of headsets
- quality of the computer's sound hard and software
- a length of cable is required for the headset
- does not work if the computer is not on
- does not feel very professional
- requires software for making, receiving and transferring calls
- software popping up on screen unexpectedly may annoy users

But the most serious issue is the fact that the committee members do not like them. They believe, understandably, that a headset is not for everyone and some potential users may be put off by this.

USB internet phones

A USB telephone uses the USB (Universal Serial Bus) socket of a computer to connect it to telephone services. It is basically a computer peripheral (just like a headset) that utilises the computer's own VOIP software like XLite to function like a VOIP telephone. The only difference between a USB telephone and a headset is that the device is made physically to look like a telephone.

As the USB phones can be connected to computers which connect to the LAN using WIFI, it can therefore operate without using physical cables to connect of the telephone system.

Typically, these phones are advertised as USB SKYPE™ phones and are compatible to most SIP or internet telephony service.

DECT phones

DECT stands for Digital Enhanced Cordless Technology; they are basically wireless telephones that generally work with standard telephone lines (PSTN). DECT phones have been available on the market for many years and have proven to be very reliable in operation whilst offering good quality calls. The advantages are:-

- good range (up to 300metres)
- good voice quality (depends on the phones)
- low cost (depending on the make and model)

On the other hand, there are issues with them too:-

- batteries are required and need to be changed occasionally
- potential to be misplaced by users
- does not operate like a business desk phone

A system based on a few standard DECT phones and a basic base station would have allowed for a wireless based telephone system without the need of a PBX. However, this type of system has very few features that a good PBX system can offer and they can only share one line. Since the project requires a business class system, standard DECT phone system will not be good enough.

Most of the DECT phone systems currently available are geared towards the consumer market; typically, they will be used for multiple handsets to share a single telephone line. In a lot of cases, these handsets will be used in different parts of the house. The use of these systems is pretty much what the project will be using it for.

For this project, the requirement is a bit higher than the standard consumer requirements though; the system needs to be designed for a small business. It will require a base station that can be connected to a LAN and used as a SIP telephone system. The handsets will be used as extensions allowing calls to be transferred between handsets as if they are standard business desktop telephones.

The Siemens Gigaset A580 IP

The A580 bases station with handsets shown below:-

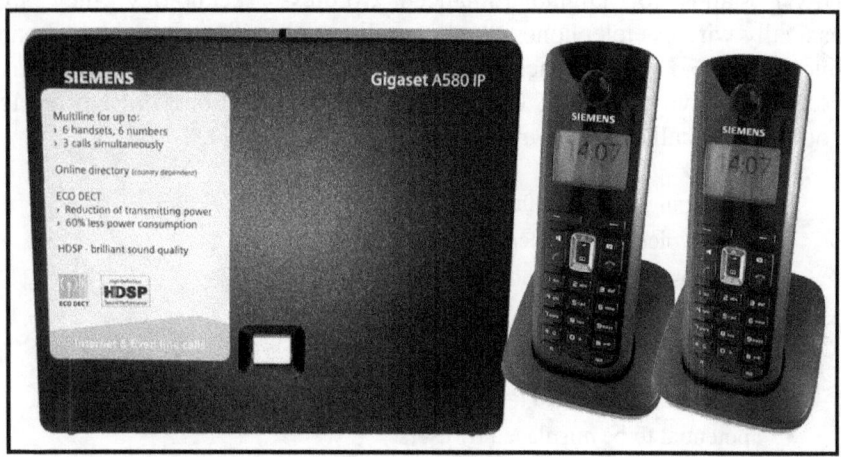

As luck would have it, George has already got such a system and he has been using it for his home. The system has been purchased a few years ago when he wanted to learn about VOIP. It has been very reliable and has always provided reasonably good quality calls, both on the landline and SIP (internet telephony).

It has just dawned on him that he has already proven that the concept of DECT is good and that the project can actually use a system similar to his. After all, he has 4 handsets located on different floors and different rooms in his house. All his handsets can use either the landline or the internet to make and receive calls. His family has been very happy with the reliability and the call quality of the system. Finally, in order for the system to work as a business class system, calls must be transferrable. A quick look at the manual of his DECT phone system reveals that it is possible to transfer calls between handsets, so his own DECT system at least, will be suitable for the project.

Proposed telephone system for the project

Whilst it is technically possible to use a DECT phone for business, one potential pitfall is that users may not like the handsets if they are used to using conventional desk phones. The question is raised with the committee members and the consensus of opinion is that everyone has a mobile phone these days and holding a DECT phone is not that different to holding a bigger mobile phone, so they do not see a problem with that.

After going on line to see what is available that fits the budget, George suddenly realised that most of the equipment is available already. First of all, the school has replaced their "Pi 2Bs" with "Pi 3s", so there are several redundant "Pi 2Bs" sitting inside the drawers of the storeroom.

Although the "Pi 2B" may not be the state of the art device to be used as a PBX, its processing power compares favourably with some of the entry level PBX devices. The "Pi 2B" has a Quad core A7 processor running at 900MHz and 1GB RAM. In comparison, the excellent Zycoo CooVox-U20 V2 uses a Dual core A7 1GHz with 512MB RAM and can support up to 15 simultaneous connections. So the expected two or three concurrent calls should not be an issue as far as processing speed is concerned. This means the project can make use of one of the free "Pi 2Bs" and the cost to the project will be nothing.

Now that's a good start for the project, what about the DECT system then? George has had the Gigaset 580 IP system for a while now, if he donates his system to the project, he can replace it with a brand new and up to date one. Having recently become a father, he has been interested in a system that is capable of room monitoring like the Gigaset N510 IP. So by offering his current system to the project and replacing it with the Gigaset 510 IP, he can kill two birds with one stone and the cost to the project thus far is still zero!

The only cost left to consider now is the 4G router. Unfortunately, George has to accept that a telephone system for nothing is not achievable for this project. So reluctantly, he has to come up with a proposal that will actually cost something for the project.

The actual system will consist of:-
- Raspberry Pi 2B as PBX
- Huawei B315 4G router for internet/SMS/mobile calls
- Gigaset 580IP DECT system for all incoming and outgoing calls
- 4 Handsets

The main office (room 1) will be the location for the "Pi", the 4G router, the Gigaset base station and two of the handsets. The "Pi" and the base station will be connected to the 4G router by a short network cable as they can be located literally within half a metre from each other.

Diagram showing locations of the handsets and equipment below:-

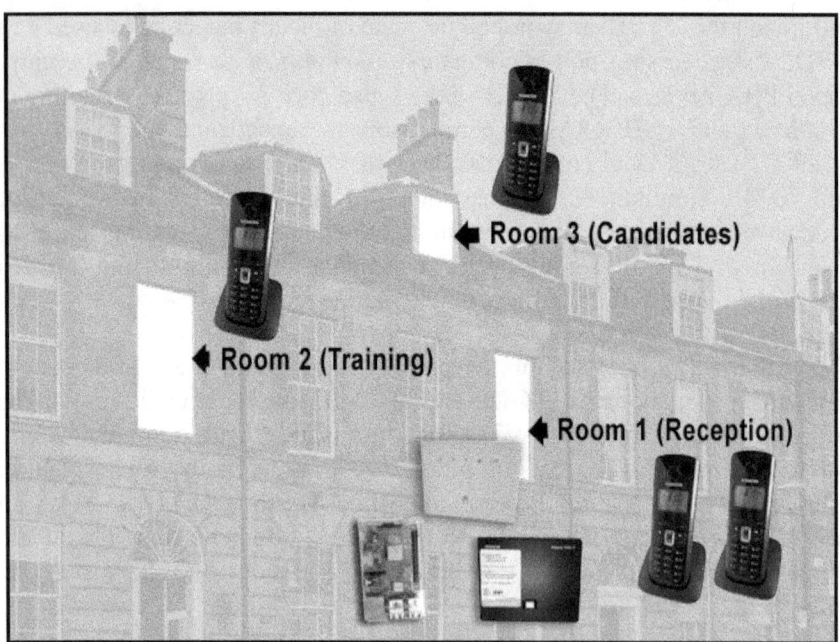

The four handsets will be located at convenient locations amongst the three rooms as shown above.

Summary of proposal

The telephone system will be able to offer business class telephony services for the project. It will have the ability to:
- have a geographical landline number with 5 lines
- receive all incoming calls using this geographical number
- make and receive concurrent calls using internet telephony
- make calls to mobiles using the SIM within the 4G router and utilise the unlimited call package
- send and receive SMS messages using the same SIM package
- transfer calls to different handsets (extensions)
- have voicemail facilities

The following diagram shows how the physical telephone system should work:-

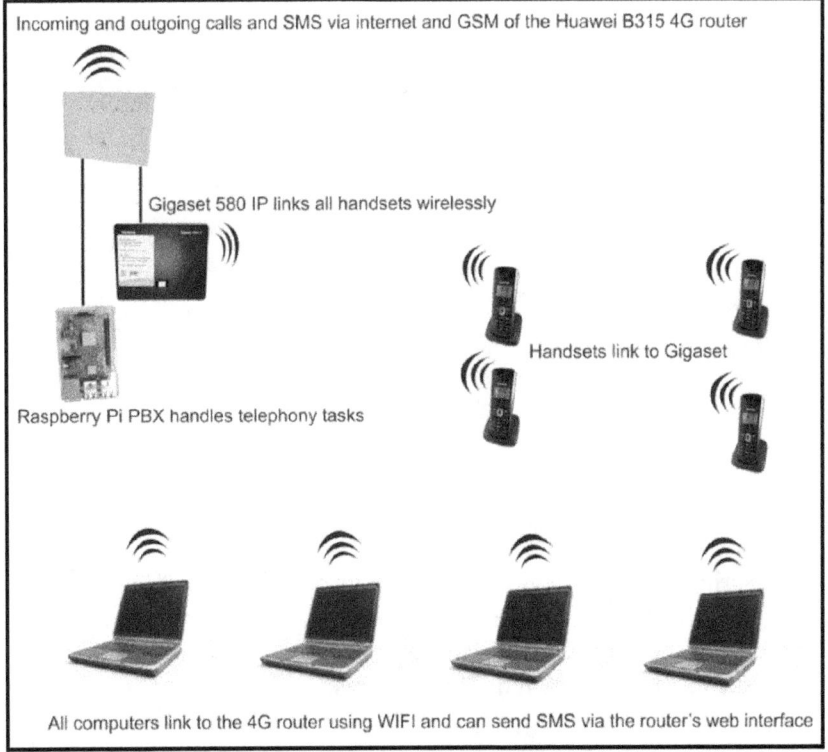

The above diagram shows that apart from two LAN cables connecting the "Pi" and the A580 to the B315, no other cabling is needed.

Since the school has agreed to donate the "Pi" to the project and the DECT system will be supplied by George himself, the only equipment cost to the project will be the 4G router at around £120 plus carriage. It is not surprising that the committee accepted the proposal immediately.

During the meeting, Jim Kinroy, whose grandson came up with the "Pi" as a PBX idea offered to purchase the 4G router and donate it to the project. So the project can now go ahead without any financial worries regarding the telephone system as all initial investments are covered.

Rear view of the Huawei B315 below:-

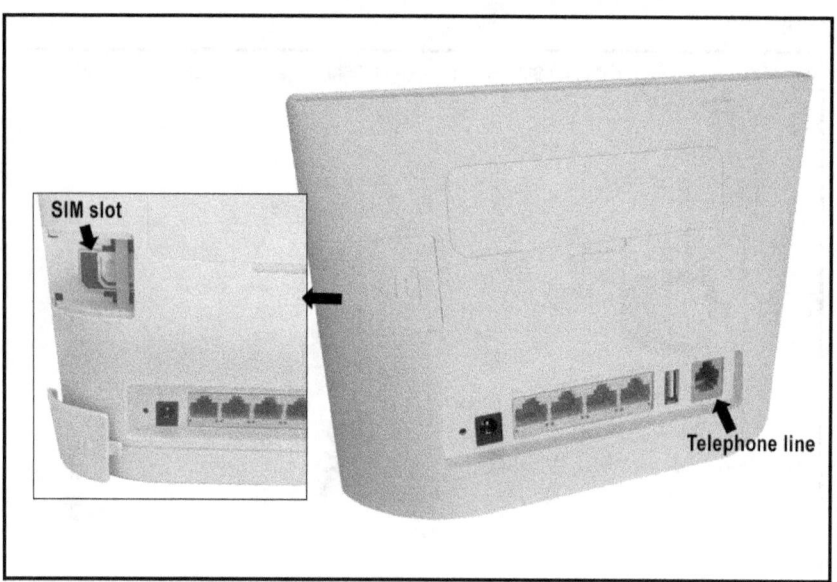

The description of the device is that it is unlocked and can support up to 32 devices via WIFI. This means that it should work with most mobile service providers in the UK and should support all the necessary devices like laptops and desktops in different rooms.

George knows that specifications are one thing, but actual operation is the only real way of proving the devices works as stated. So an order is placed with an online vender for the device and it arrives a couple of days later.

The B315 looks almost exactly the same as most routers on the market with the exception of an extra compartment for a SIM a USB socket and the telephone socket.

It is obvious where everything should be plugged in, so it is literally ready to work straight out the box. At this stage, it would be tempting to just plug everything in and start, however, experience tells George that he should just be patient and do things in logical stages.

SIM installation

A "Pay as you go" SIM from the mobile provider Three is purchased for testing purpose as "Three" seems to provide good signals and has the most suitable package for the project. Since it is often necessary for a SIM to be activated correctly before first use, it is best to install the SIM into a normal mobile phone first and follow instructions from the mobile provider. After doing so, a test call is made to make sure that the SIM is activated and is ready to be installed into the B315.

After the SIM is installed, the router is powered up and ready to be used. George plugs a standard telephone to the telephone socket to test if it works, a test call is made to confirm that it does and the quality is good, so stage one is completed.

4G internet connection

Since the router has 4 LAN sockets, a laptop is plugged into the router via a network cable for this test. The reason for using a cable connection is to eliminate any WIFI issues during the testing process.

The laptop is set to acquire its network settings automatically, the hope is that it will acquire its network settings from the B315 router and just work. To George's amazement, opening a browser window brings up the browsers default homepage! Changing the URL to another website loads it up almost immediately. The B315 appears to have worked perfectly with the "Three" SIM without any need for configuration. A quick speed test shows that the speed as around 30Mb downloads and around 20Mb upload.

George is very surprised, as in his experience, most equipment only works after proper configuration and often requires a bit is tweaking. But this seems to just work out the box. He thinks that is because the B315 was ordered from a UK supplier and it is pre-configured for UK mobile providers.

Setting up the B315

It is time now to look at the configurations and settings of the B315 and may be modifying it to be more appropriate for the project if necessary. The B315 is pre-configured with the default ip address of 192.168.8.1. The log in screen of the B315 can be opened by typing in 192.168.8.1 in the address bar of the laptop's browser.

Accessing the initial screen with a browser

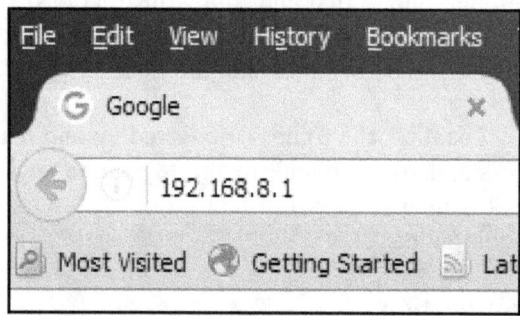

To access the web GUI, type in the default IP address as shown above

The Home screen if the B315 is displayed, showing that it is connected to 3 via 4G and has it signal strength of 3 bars.

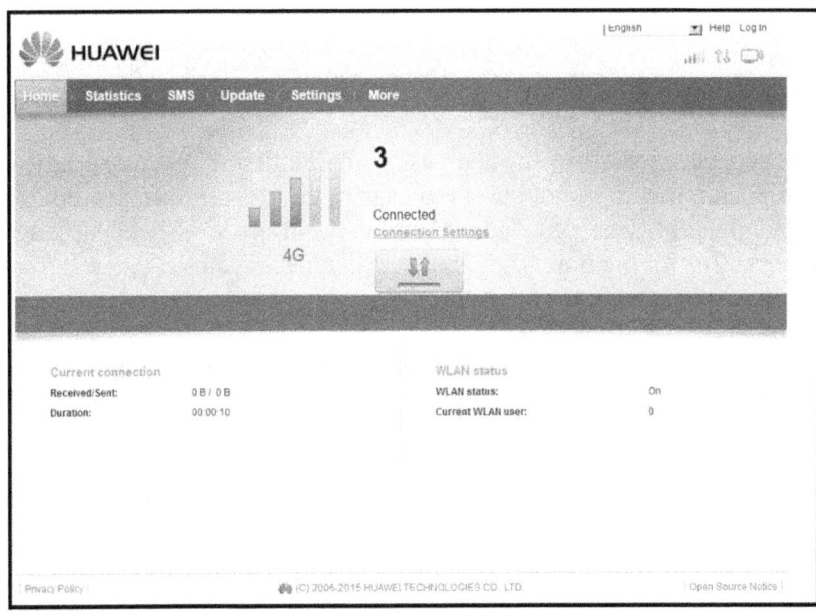

By clicking Log in on the top left of the browser window, the log in screen now appears.

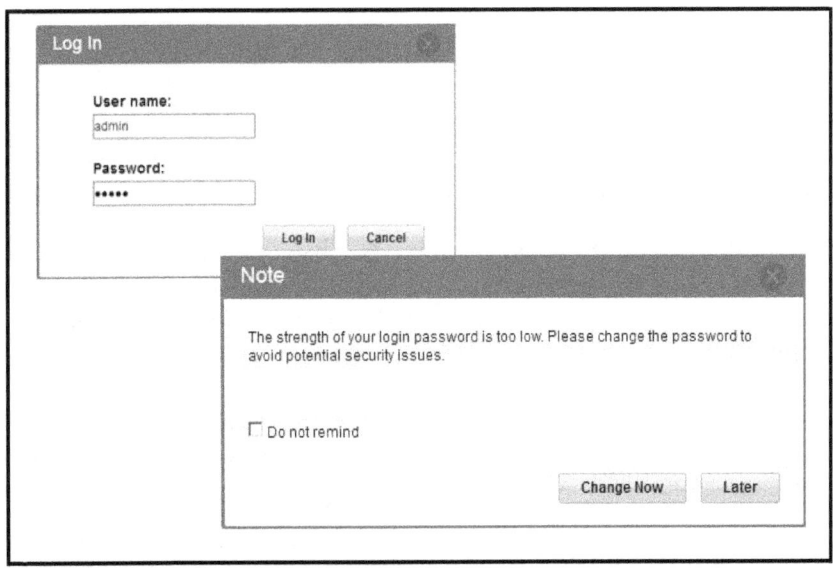

By using the default username "admin" and the default password "admin", the settings of the B315 are now accessible and ready to be modified.

After typing in the username and password, the first thing that appears on screen is an alert to remind users to change the password to a strong one as the default password "admin" is very insecure. Clicking "Later" bypasses this for the time being, but it will appear again on the next log in so users do not forget to change the default password.

So in the interest of security, the password must be changed. George decides to make this change later as there are other modifications to be changed anyway.

A quick check of the setting shows that the SIM in the B315 has been correctly recognised and is working.

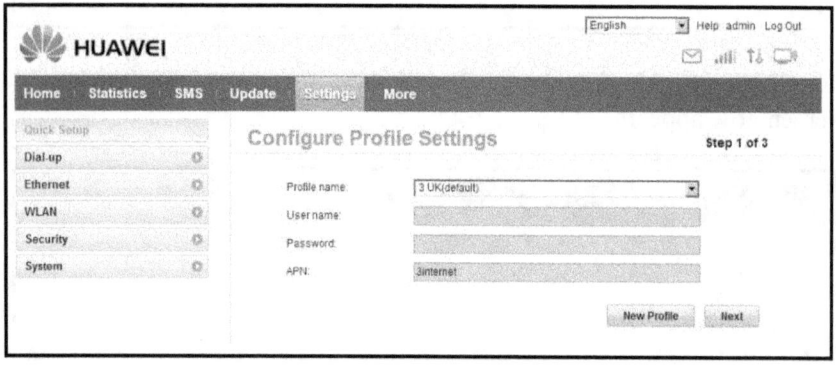

The first thing to do is to note down the WIFI settings. He is interested in particular, the WPA pre-shared key, which can also be found on the bottom of the B315 itself together with the SSID. He checks the key carefully against the printed label at the bottom of the B315.

Experience tells him that the password of the printed label of some routers has been known to be incorrect, thus making WIFI connections to them impossible.

WIFI settings page of the B315

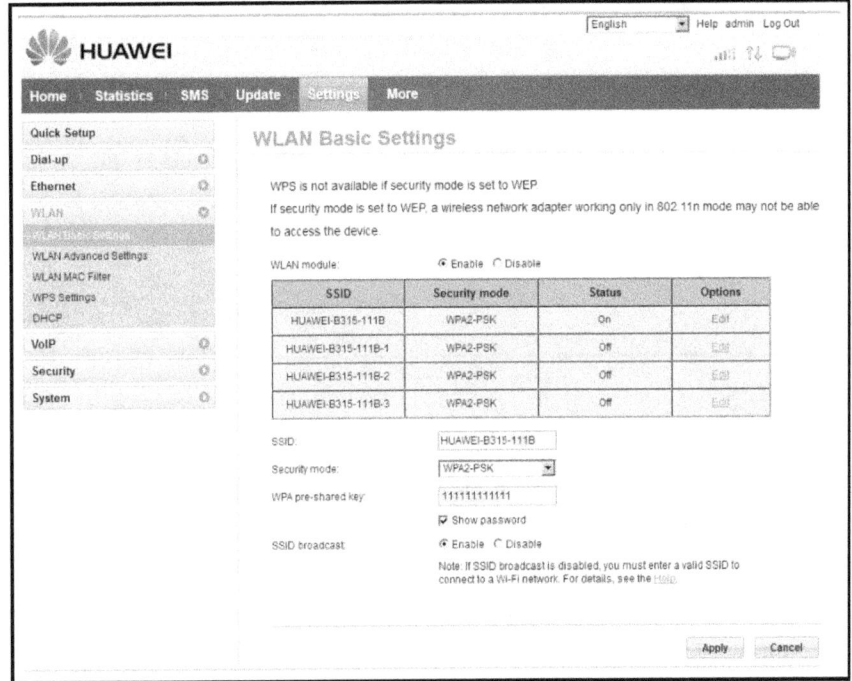

Changing the log in password

The password is changed at the "Modify Password page" and is changed to a very secured one which includes upper, lower case, numbers and a couple of special symbols. When the Password strength is indicated as "High", the password is noted down and saved.

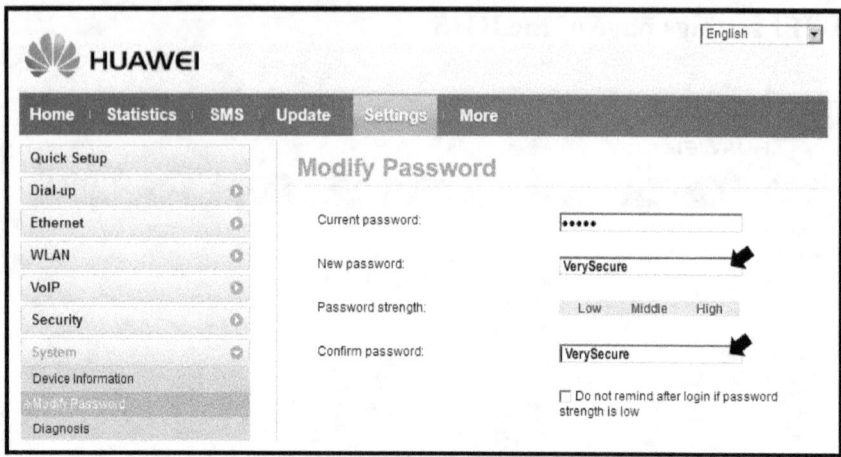

SMS test

To test the facilities for sending and receiving SMS texts, click on the "SMS" tab. To send a new text, click on the "New Message" button.

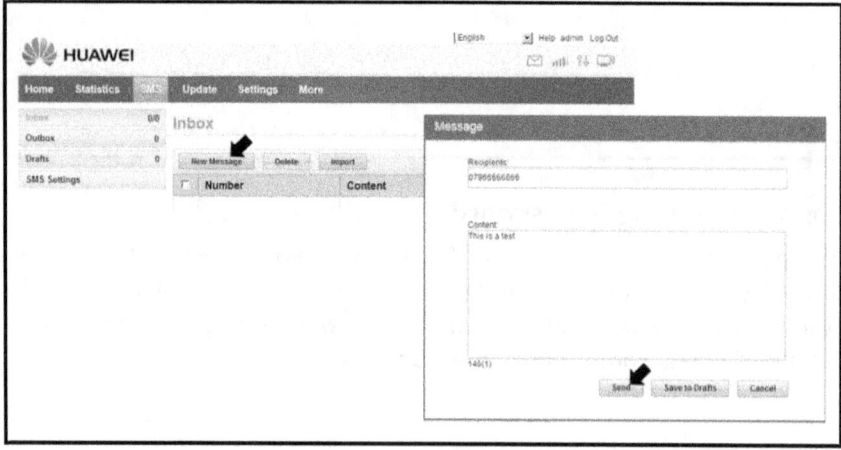

The "Message" pop up window appears, type the mobile number of the recipient in the "Recipients:" tab and the message in the "Contents" section. Click "send" to send the SMS.

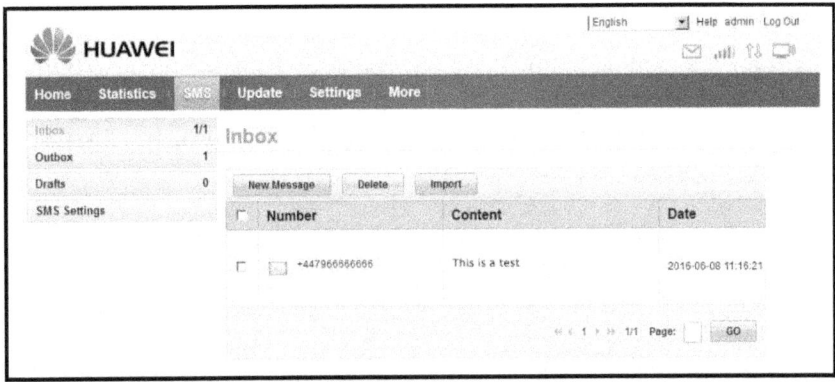

Within a few seconds, the SMS is received by the test recipient, a reply is sent back to the number of SIM in the B315. A few seconds later, the reply appears in the "Inbox". So the test for sending and receiving SMS text is completely successfully and it works exactly as expected.

Check for relevant Updates

The B315 firmware can be updated if required, it is done by clicking the "Update" button.

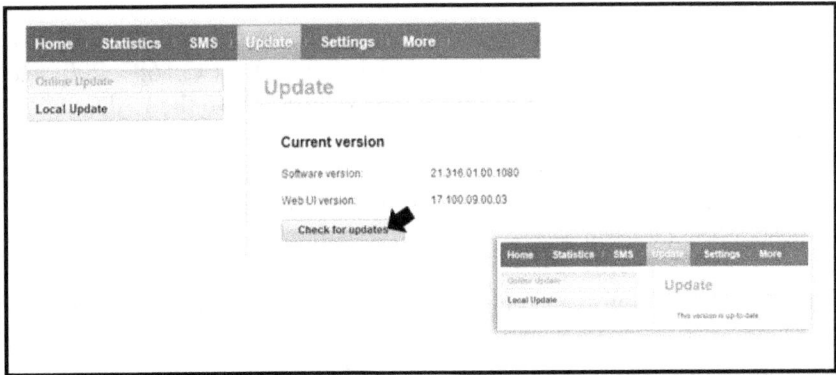

Click "Check for Updates" button to see if there are any relevant updates, the B315 firmware is up to date.

DHCP settings

This is an optional step, however, George knows that his Gigaset DECT system is already assigned with a static address of 192.168.2.180, he decides to change the address scheme of the B315 to 192.168.2.x just to save him changing the Gigaset later.

To change the DHCP settings, click WLAN and then DHCP.

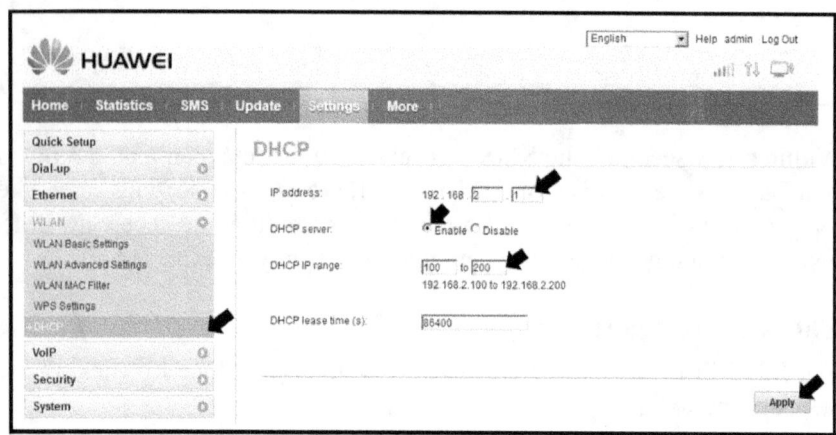

The IP address of the B315 is changed to 192.168.2.1 and the DHCP IP range the B315 will assign is from 192.168.2.100 - 192.168.2.200. This should be more than sufficient for all the devices within the LAN.

After applying the changes, the B315 is restarted. Since the B315 will have an IP address of 192.168.2.1, from now on, this address will have to be used to log in again.

While the b315 is in the process of restarting, the laptop is also restarted just so that it can release its current network settings and acquire a new set from the B315.

After the laptop has restarted, the "ipconfig" command is run from the command prompt and the following display confirms that DHCP is working correctly on the B315 and the laptop has acquired its new network settings.

```
C:\Windows\System32>ipconfig

Windows IP Configuration

Ethernet adapter Local Area Connection 4:

   Connection-specific DNS Suffix  . :
   Link-local IPv6 Address . . . . . : fe81::315d:5d17:b117:2111%21
   IPv4 Address. . . . . . . . . . . : 192.168.2.100
   Subnet Mask . . . . . . . . . . . : 255.255.255.0
   Default Gateway . . . . . . . . . : 192.168.2.1
```

Opening a browser window displays the home page and a quick search confirms that the network is working and the laptop is connected to the internet and is operating fine.

The second laptop with WIFI capabilities is used to identify and connect to the B315 by using the correct "SSID" and the "WPA key". This confirms that the WIFI functions are working.

There are some other features which may be potentially useful, but the main function of utilising the capabilities of this device has been satisfied. For the project, George decides that there is no need to modify any more settings as everything required for the internet and telephone system appears to be functioning correctly.

As far as the project is concerned, the requirements are:

- internet access without a telephone line
- mobile calls using the SIM package
- SMS text using the SIM package

The above requirements have all been met; all that is left now is to configure the "Pi" to act as a PBX to offer internet telephony services to the project users.

Setting up the "Pi"

Although George has set up a "Pi" as a PBX for the school project before, it was over a year ago, so he decides to do a bit of research to update his knowledge first. He is particularly impressed by an article on the web at "http://nerdvittles.com/?p=17094". This article describes all the stages required in setting up a "Pi" with Incredible PBX™ and Raspian 8 Jessie. This means it is possible to download and install all required software in one go for free.

Incredible PBX™ as its name suggests is an open-source PBX server software based on the very popular Asterisk 13®. It is an open-source framework for building communications applications which powers hundreds of thousands of IP PBX servers all over the world. As his previous school project is also based on the Asterisk®, he is very comfortable with this idea.

Raspian 8 Jessie is the latest operating system based on Debian Linux for the "Pi", and the different versions of Debian are named after characters from the "Toy Story" films. The latest stable version of Debian is named Jessie, the cow girl character in "Toy Story 2".

Although the names of the main components sound like child's play and the software is open-sourced, George knows that these are serious and professional standard software, the fact that Asterisk® is being used by numerous organisations all over the world bear testament to how good it really is.

The next stage is to download and install the software on the "Pi". Before doing that, it is worth seriously considering the security implications first. In general, a firewall should be used to protect the PBX from hacking which can allow hackers to make calls on the project's expense.

The recommendations are:-

- Preconfigured IPtables Linux Firewall
- Preconfigured Travelin' Man 3 WhiteLists
- Randomized Port Knocker for Remote Access
- TM4 WhiteListing by Telephone (optional)
- Fail2Ban Log Monitoring for SSH, Apache, Asterisk
- Randomized Ultra-Secure Passwords
- Automatic Update Utility for Security & Bug Fixes
- Asterisk Manager Lockdown to localhost
- Apache htaccess Security for Vulnerable Web Apps
- Security Alerts via RSS Feeds in Kennonsoft and Incredible PBX™

For the purpose of the project, security is not necessarily of the highest importance. Obviously, secured passwords for all parts of the system is absolutely a must.

The PBX therefore should be configured so that it is:-

- not accessible from outside the LAN
- with very secured passwords for management of all devices
- can only make calls that are covered by prepaid packages

Other related issues to address are:-

- limiting the number of simultaneous calls
- no premium numbers and international calls
- landline call package to include only local, national and certain non-geographical "08" numbers
- a small amount prepaid to cover non-geographical numbers
- SIM package can only be used to dial mobile numbers (07)
- placing the "Pi" behind a firewall (B315)

As luck would have it, by using 4G internet access, some security issues has already been inadvertently addressed. One of the main issues with using mobile broadband is the fact that mobile operators use CGNAT (carrier grade network address translation) to allow for the larger numbers of users on their network. In effect, the mobile providers share every IP address they allocate amongst several users.

As it is not possible to identify the real IP address of the B315, its "Port Forwarding" function will not work. This means external access to a user's internal LAN is almost impossible, since the external IP address allocated to the user is not unique - it is shared between many other users. This creates headaches for users requiring remote access to the LAN, but adds security to the system. Unfortunately, it will also mean remote extensions for the project's PBX will not be possible.

In order to turn the "Pi" into a fully functional PBX, it is necessary for it to have an operating system and the PBX server software installed and configured. Since the article by nerdvittles.com shows both Raspian 8 and Incredible PBX™ can be downloaded and installed at the same time, it seems to be the best approach. The stages described are as follows:-

- download the relevant image file
- extract the file to local file system
- burn the image to a micro SD card
- boot up the "Pi" configure it

Downloading the file

Summary	Files	Reviews	Support	Wiki	Feature Requests	Discussion

Looking for the latest version? Download IncrediblePBX13.2.iso (890.2 MB)

Home / IncrediblePBX13-Raspbian8 for Raspberry Pi 2+3

Name	Modified	Size	Downloads / Week	
↑ Parent folder				
readme.txt	2016-03-09	1.5 kB	17	ⓘ
incrediblepbx13-raspbian8-gvoauth.zip	2016-03-08	1.5 GB	104	ⓘ
incrediblepbx13-raspbian8.zip	2016-03-07	1.5 GB	85	ⓘ
incrediblefax13-raspbian8.tar.gz	2016-03-07	13.4 kB	3	ⓘ
Totals: 4 Items		3.0 GB	209	

Download zip file incrediblepbx13-raspian8.zip as shown above:-

Extracting the files
Extract all files in the zip file to local file system e.g. c:\pi_pbx

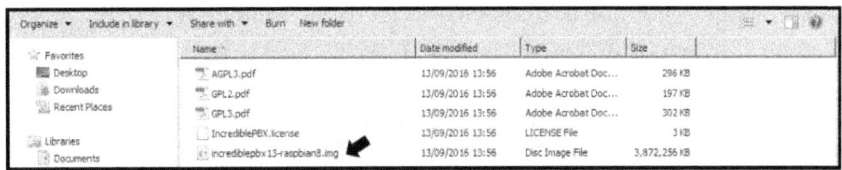

The image required is incrediblepbx13-raspian8.img

Writing the image to a microSD card
Many different software can be used to write the downloaded image to the microSD card to be used for the "Pi". George has decided to use an open-source software "Win32DiskImager".

The software can be downloaded at :-
https://sourceforge.net/projects/win32diskimager/.

Once "Win32DiskImager" is downloaded and installed, run the program to write the image to the microSD card. Run "Win32DiskImager"

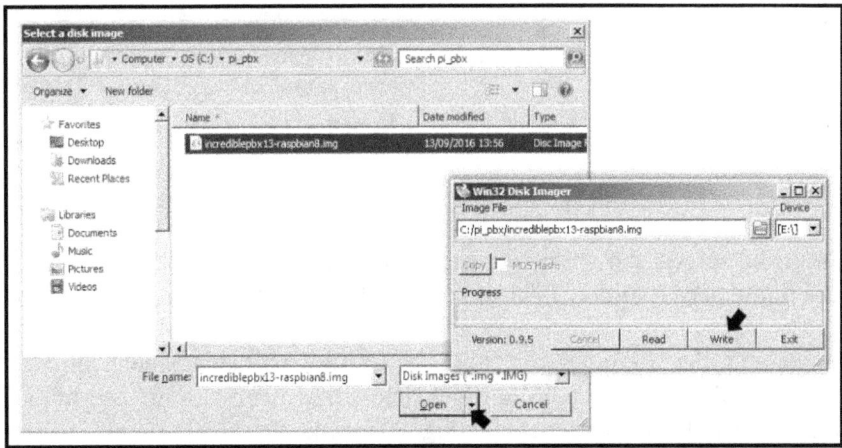

Page 43

Click "Open" and select the correct .img file and then click "Write" to write image to Device E:\ (microSD card)

Once the process is completed, insert the microSD card into the correct slot on the "Pi". A keyboard is then connected to one of the USB ports and an HDMI monitor is connected to the HDMI port and the "Pi" is now ready for the set up and configuration process.

Once the "Pi" is powered up, a log in screen will be displayed. Log in by using the default username "pi" and the default password "raspberry". Then agree to the licensing terms and continue.

When the "Pi" powers up, it will have acquired its IP address from the B315, whilst it is possible to identify the IP address allocated by the B315, it is sensible to note down the IP address first. This saves the trouble of having to look for the IP address of the "Pi" later on when it comes to configuring it.

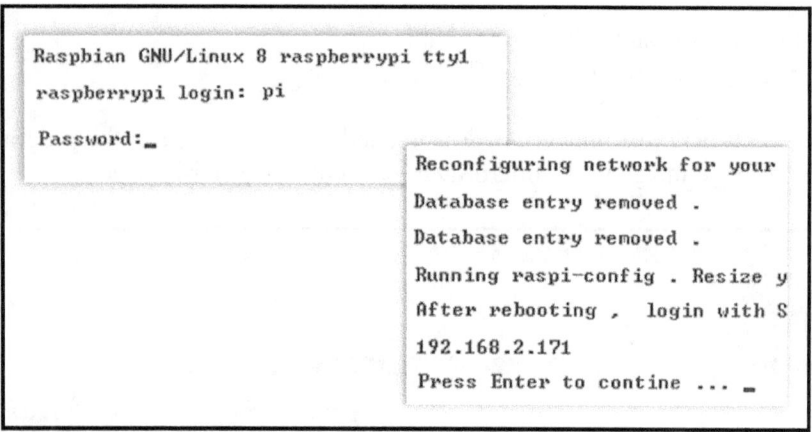

From the screen shown above, the IP address of 192.168.2.171 is noted and future access to the "Pi" can be made by using this address.

By default, the "Pi" uses port 9001 for secure web management. In order to access the "Pi" for configuration later, it is necessary to use https://192.168.2.171:9001 to access the log in screen.

Access to manage the Incredible PBX™ can be done by omitting the "s" in the "https" and the port number of 9001 i.e. http://192.168.2.171.

Once the IP address of the "Pi" has been recorded, the set up process continues and after a restart, the following screen appears:-

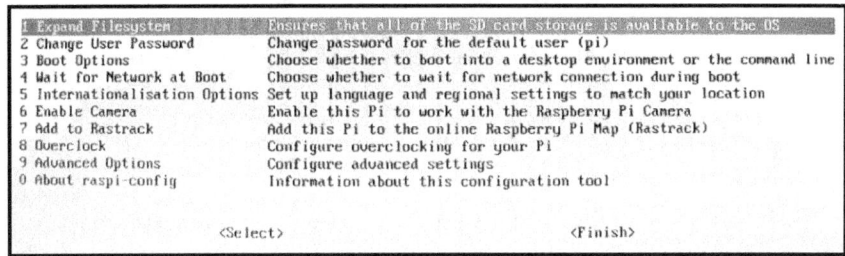

Choosing the first option allows the available space on the microSD card to be fully utilised, press "Enter" to execute and "OK" to continue.

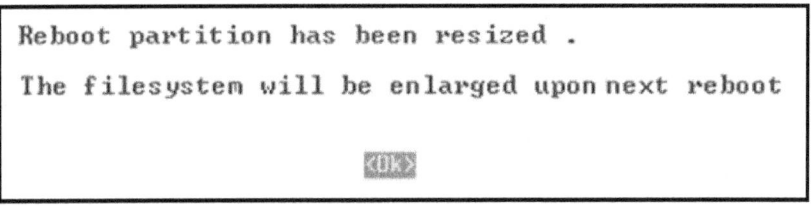

Next, choose option 2 to change the password of the default user "pi". Choose a strong password of at lease 8 characters with a combination of upper/lower case as well as numbers and symbols.

Page 45

Once the "Pi" has been restarted, the "Pi" will continue and prompt for changing of the "Pi" and "Unix" password. This will be followed by:

```
FreePBX admin password is just as critical as your root password.
Enter new FreePBX admin password for RaspPi 2/3: VerySecure
FreePBX admin password: Unjai16

Enter new ARI admin password for RaspPi 2/3: VerySecure
ARI admin password: VerySecure

A default extension (701) has been created with Incredible PBX.
Anyone with your extension password can make calls on your nickel.
Enter new password for extension 701 on RaspPi 2/3: VerySecure
Extension 701 password: VerySecure

Enter email address for delivery of ext. 701 voicemails: admin@project.org.uk
Extension 701 email delivery address: admin@project.org.uk

Enter NUMERIC password for ext. 701 voicemail access: 276701
Extension 701 voicemail password: 276701

Reminders web access is protected by Apache admin password
AsteriDex web access is protected by Apache admin password
phpMyAdmin web access is protected by Apache admin password
Enter new Apache admin password for your server: VerySecure
Apache admin password will be set to: VerySecure

Telephone reminders can also be created by dialing 123 from any phone.
With your Reminders password, anyone can set up calls to anywhere.
Enter NUMERIC password for Telephone Reminders access: 276701
Telephone Reminders (dial 123) access password: 276701

If these are correct, press any key to continue or ctrl-C to exit_
```

Record all the passwords used, it is extremely important to use secure passwords for all devices and settings. "NUMERIC" passwords are required for accessing "Extension voicemails" and "Telephone Reminders". As access to these services is usually by using the dial pad of the telephone, it is sensible to use only numbers. Once all passwords have been noted, continue until the process is completed.

Change Time Zone

It is extremely important to change the "Time Zone" to match UK time, if "Time Zone" is not set correctly, it will need to be changed later as all voicemail timings will be incorrect. Under "Internationalisation Options", choose options as shown below:-

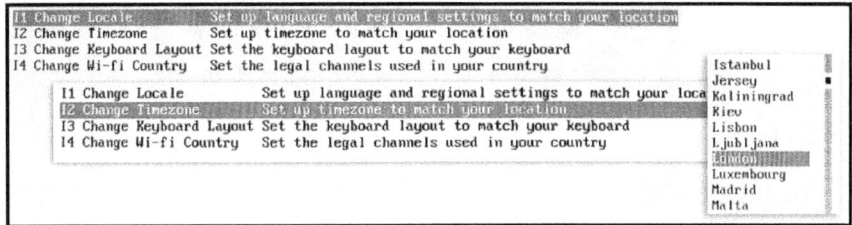

Click "OK" to continue, all the other choices are optional as the main component for the telephone system is Incredible PBX™ which can be accessed via its web interface.

Once completed, the "Web admin" can be accessed by using a browser from a computer on the LAN at https://192.168.2.171:9001. Log in by using credentials specified earlier.

The front screen displays the system status, it shows that the "Pi" appears to be using the wrong time zone and there are many updates available.

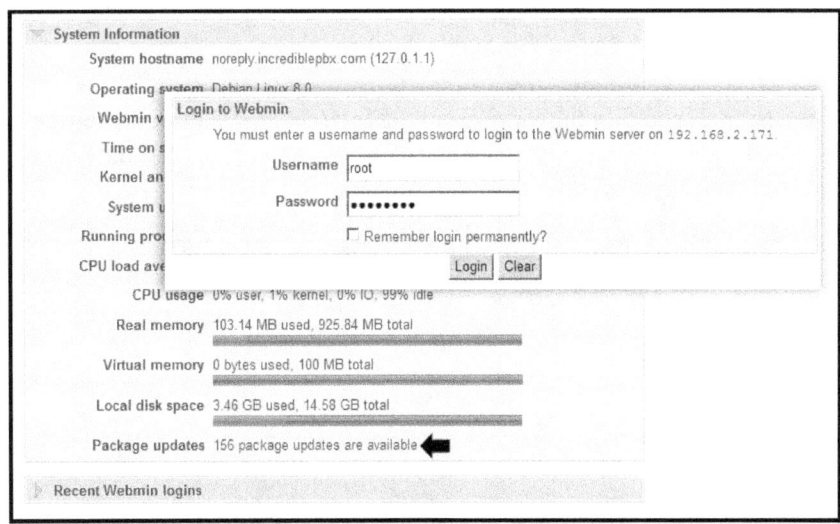

First thing to do is to run all the updates as it is crucial to keep the "Pi" up to date and secure. After all updates are applied, change the time zone to Europe/London to match the project location.

On the left hand side of the screen, choose "Hardware" > "System time",

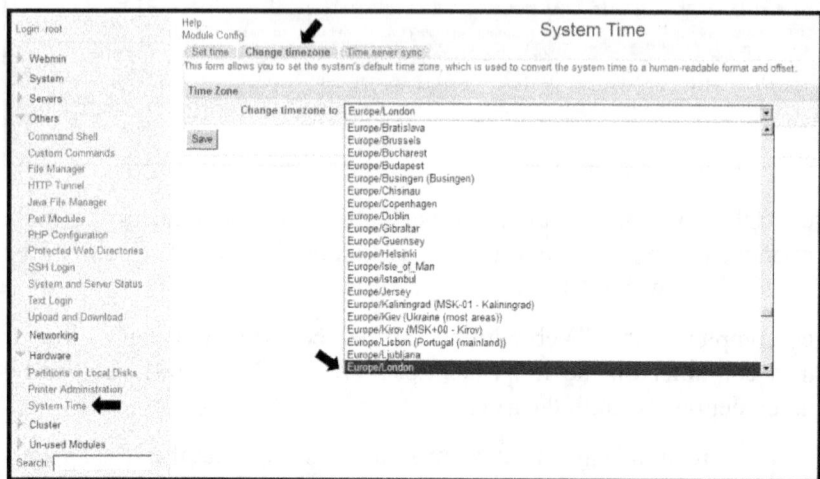

Click the "Change timezone" tab and choose "Change timezone to" "Europe/London" as shown above.

If necessary, specify a time server on the internet to synchronise timing with under the "Time server sync" tab. Choose an appropriate time server e.g. *server 0.europe.pool.ntp.org*

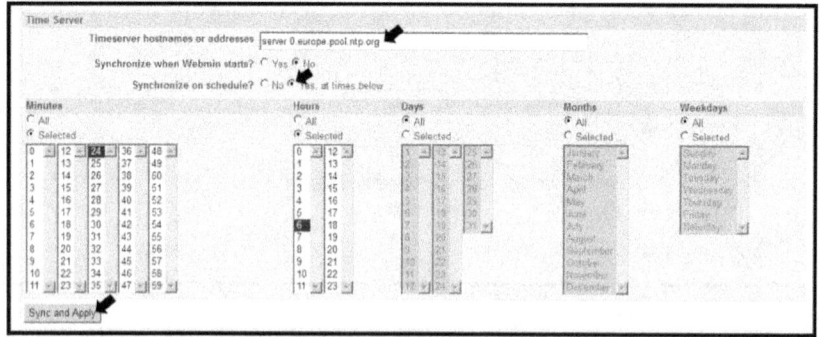

Click "Sync and Apply" to apply the settings. Check and make sure the time displayed at the status screen is correct. By now, the "Incredible PBX™" is ready; to access the user interface, go to http://192.168.2.171.

Setting up the PBX

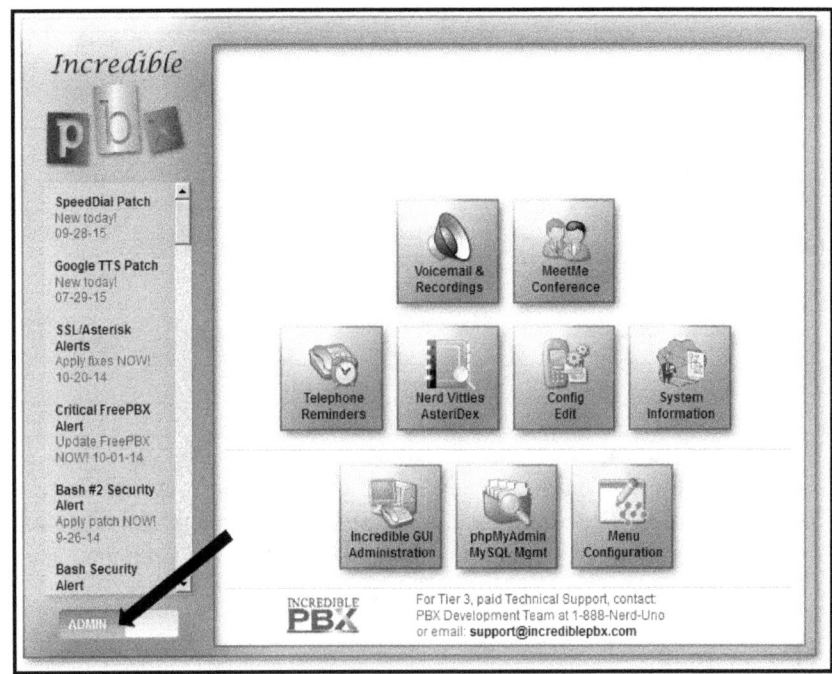

The initial screen displayed is for standard user login; click the "ADMIN" button on the left to log in as administrator.

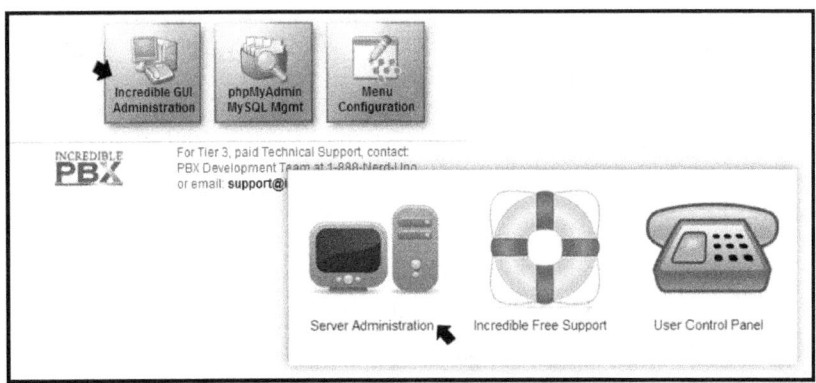

Click "Incredible GUI Administration and then click "Server Administration" to continue.

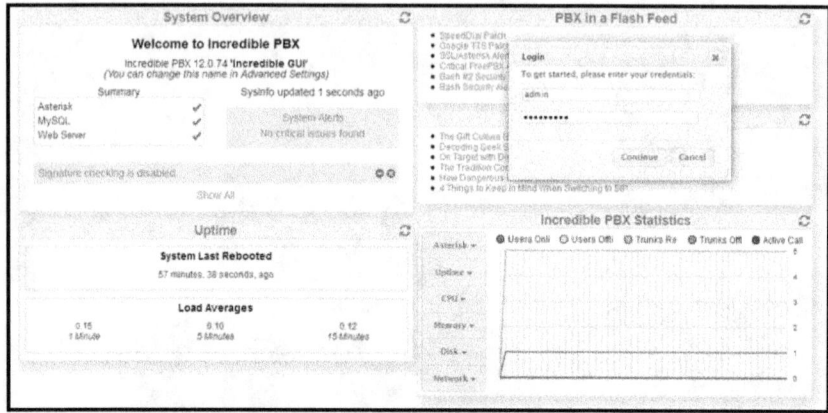

Log in using the credential already noted down in the previous stage. A "Welcome Screen" appears; displaying "System Overview" together with a few status sections. If "Updates" are available, do so to keep the system up to date and secure.

So far so good

Looking at the status of the various sections, everything appears to be running according to plan up to this point. The two main devices have been operating correctly. So far, the B315 has been:-

- operating correctly as an 4G internet /WIFI/LAN router
- able to send and receive SMS
- able to make and receive calls using a mobile SIM and standard telephone

For the "Pi"

- Raspian 8 (Debian Linux 8.0) has been installed
- Incredible PBX™ has been installed

Configuring outgoing emails

By default, the system is configured to use Exim4 as MTA (Mail Transfer Agent). Exim4 is configured to directly send mail to the recipient's email servers. Unfortunately these days, most mail servers will block emails from email servers using dynamic IP addresses. As the project will be using 4G mobile service with a dynamically assigned IP address, this will almost certainly happen. Since the "Pi" will be using Exim4 to send voicemails as email attachments out to the relevant recipients, these voicemails will probably be blocked by the recipients' own mail service providers.

To overcome this, the "Pi" will have to use a smart host (relay host) to relay and deliver the voicemails to the recipients. Since the project already uses an internet service provider for their website and emails, the mail server of the provider will be used as the smart host. The mail server name is mail.project.org.uk (a made up name only) will be used by Exim4 in the smart host configuration later.

To configure Exim4, it is necessary to log directly (not via "Web admin") into the "Pi" as root and the secured password set up earlier. The command to run configuration is shown below:-

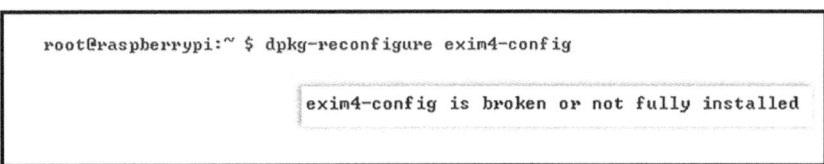

To George's surprise, an error is encountered, it looks like Exim4 is probably not fully installed by default; this means he has to install Exim4 again. The command to install Exim4 is "*apt-get –y install exim4*". Once Exim4 is installed, re-run the command "*dpkg-reconfigure exim4-config*" again.

The following screen appears:-

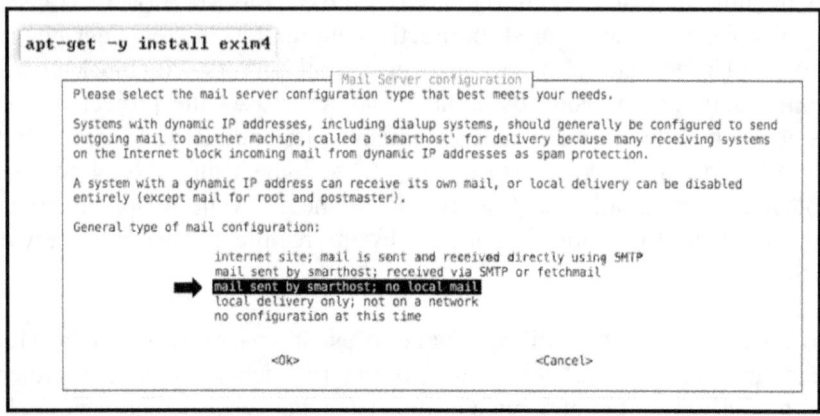

Choose sent by "smarthost; no local mail". Since the "Pi" will not be used as a mail server for the LAN, there is no need to configure other options. On the following pages just keep the default values by pressing enter, until you reach the page starting with "Please enter the IP address or the host name of a mail server". Enter the smart host and not IP address of the mail server "mail.project.org.uk". Complete the settings by just using all default values.

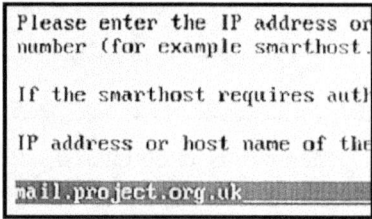

The PBX is now ready to use the specified smarthost to relay voicemails to the relevant recipients. However, it is not quite finished yet, there are still more configurations to complete although they can be done by logging into the "Webadmin" as "root" at https://192.168.2.171:9001.

In order to use the mail service provider's mail server, the sender must log in with the relevant credentials. To do so, these credentials must be included in the "passwd.client" file. On the left hand side of the screen, click "Others" > File manager > etc > exim4.

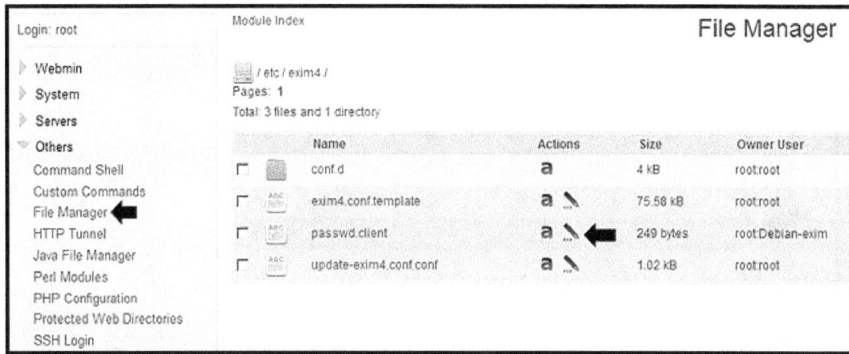

Click the editor icon to edit the file, enter the credentials as show below:-

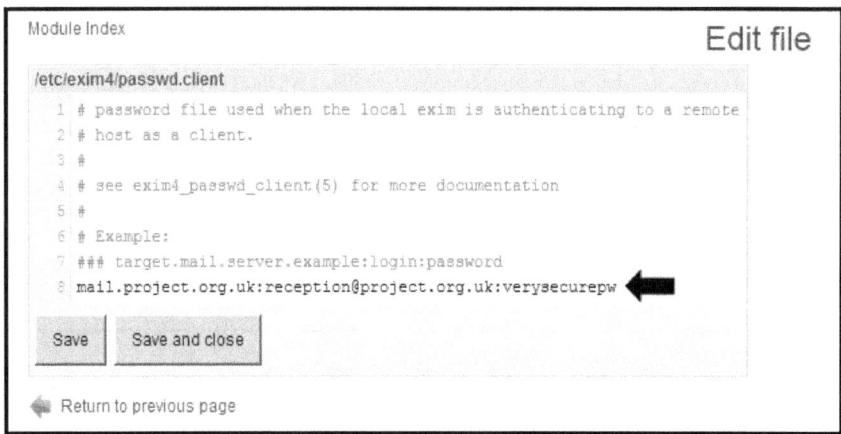

There is an optional file to edit if required. It is possible to change the email addresses of the senders of emails from the "Pi". Some email providers also require the sender addresses to the ones that are identical to the ones of the public email addresses of that account.

In this case, editing of the email-addresses file will be required; the file can be located in the "etc" folder and can be edited just like the "passwd.client" file. See the following:-

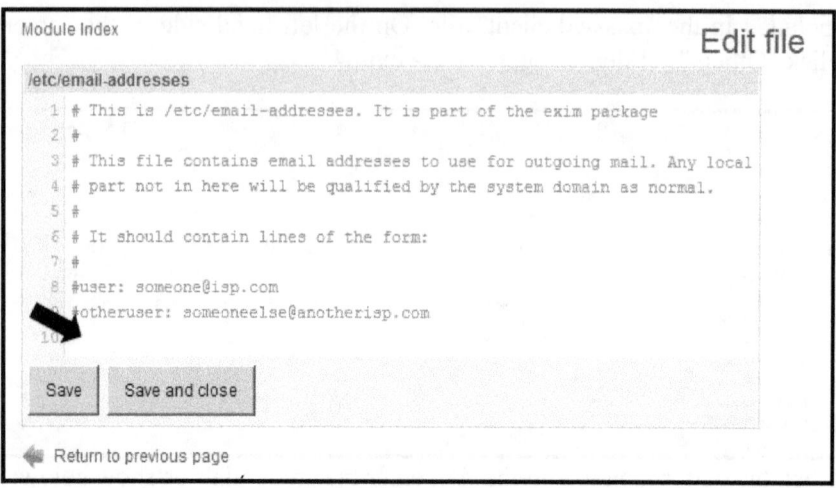

For example: root: reception@project.org.uk or asterisk: reception@project.org.uk

However, George thinks it is not necessary as this is not required by the mail service provider. In addition, this may confuse the users who may think voicemails may have been sent by the receptionist.

Once the "passwd.client" file has been edited, the changes must be activated by running the command "update-exim4.conf". This can be done in the "Command shell" as follows:-

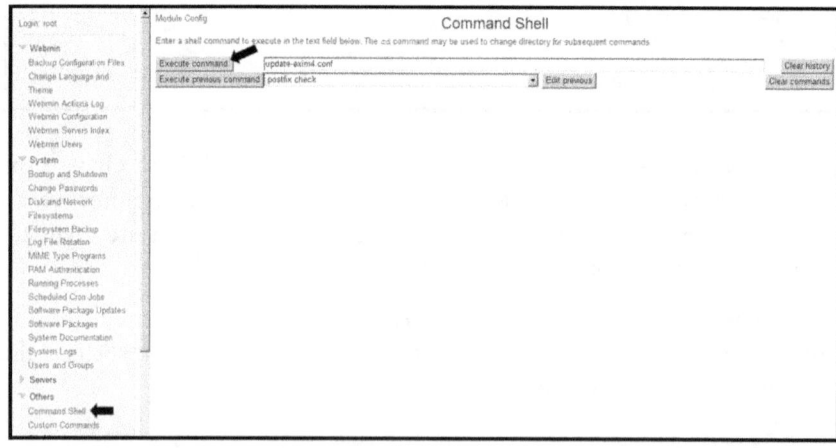

After the update is completed, a test email is sent to confirm that the settings are correct and that emails are being sent. The command to send the test is:-

echo "test message" | mail -s testmessage reception@project.org.uk.

It is shown below:-

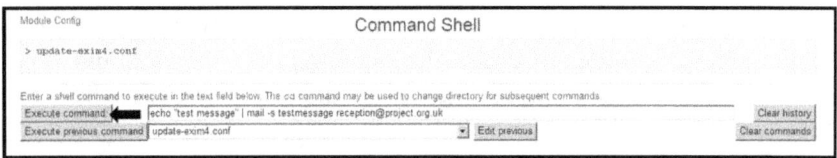

The test emails arrives at the inbox of reception. This confirms that emails are correctly relayed by the provider's mail server.

By now, George is confident that both the operating system and the PBX server are working correctly. He now has everything he needs to produce a working telephone system for the project. The planning for the management committee requirements can now proceed and this will result in how the PBX is configured.

Telephone System requirements

At the beginning of the planning of this project, the management committee has no great expectations of the telephone system at all; they just hoped that the existing telephone system in the proposed original premises worked. However, as those premises are no longer available, those low expectations have become irrelevant.

A meeting is held by the committee to set out the telephony requirements for the project in order to utilise the capabilities of the "Pi" and B315. During the meeting, a lot of interesting and useful requests has been discussed.

Management committee contacts

The most important point involves the contact details of two of the management committee members. They are both involved in other businesses; they will only be based at the project office when necessary. Since they will be heavily involved with the day to day running of the project, it will be extremely desirable for them to be easily contactable both externally and internally.

Although they are contactable on their mobile phones, they do not want their personal numbers to be available to the general public. They need something better than for the project reception to take messages and relaying these messages to them. So the committee wants a way for calls to these members to be directed to their business numbers (they both run home based businesses) so they can deal with the matters immediately.

Some of the committee members are impressed with the professional appearance of telephone voice menus of some organisations and wants to include this feature in the requirements. Although some members consider this to be a bit "over the top" for a small project, it makes sense to everyone as it would make it possible for external callers to press a number to have the calls forwarded to the relevant management committee member. This will allow the members to deal with the matter directly rather than having to wait for the message to reach them later.

Least cost routing

As the B315 has a standard landline port that utilises the SIM package for unlimited mobile calls, all outbound calls to mobiles should be routed through this line. According to the management committee, it is unlikely that there will be more than a couple of dozen calls to mobiles each day, so one line should be adequate. This should mean that all mobile calls will be covered by the SIM package.

As for local and national calls, they should be routed through the chosen SIP provider. As all these calls are covered by the provider's unlimited package, calls to all local and national numbers will be included in the package.

The only business related numbers that are not covered by any call packages are non-geographical numbers i.e. numbers that starts with 084 or 087 and VOIP numbers starting with 056. In order to cover these calls, a small amount of credit of £20 will be purchased in order to cover these calls.

All international and premium rate numbers will be barred from the being made from the system.

As long as the system is secured, only calls to approved numbers can be made. This will make budgeting for telephony costs much easier. In the unlikely event that the system is hacked, the damage will only be limited to the prepaid credit of up to £20.

General and personal voicemail as email attachments

The committee members like the idea of voicemails as email attachments because the actual messages are recorded and can be filed if necessary. In addition, since the voicemail can be replayed or forwarded to someone else, the accuracy of the message is also preserved. So it is decided that there should be voicemail facilities for the two relevant management committee members and one for reception.

Out of hours call handling

The PBX can be configured to deal with calls differently at different times, it is decided that out of hours calls will be forwarded to the extension voicemail of reception. The same process will apply to weekend and holiday calls. The receptionist will then be responsible to forward all voicemails to the correct recipients.

From the original expectation of just having a telephone system that can make, receive and transfer calls; the project can now expect a business class telephone system that is capable of:-

- "Interactive Voice Prompt" functions
- external calls forwarded to relevant management committee member
- least cost routing of calls
- voicemail as email attachments
- out of hours handling of call
- potential for improvements later

Before the committee members get too carried away, George has to manage their expectations by pointing out there are weaknesses to this telephone system too. The system is:-

- not a full VOIP system and hence does not have all the functions
- the DECT side and the standard VOIP side are not integrated
- the individual handsets are not individual extensions
- transferring of calls outside the DECT system may be difficult
- expansion of the system will not be easy

Despite the potential drawbacks of this system, the committee members are well impressed with what the system can do. The fact that it is acquired at next to no cost just adds icing to the cake.

George is going to make a list of what the members want and then to configure the "PBX" to work accordingly.

Configuring the PBX

The next stage is to configure the PBX to fulfill all the necessary requirements listed in the previous chapter. First of all, the system requires users and extensions to begin with.

Extensions

As required by the committee, there will be at least 3 extensions as follows:-

- Anne for the employment section
- Susan for the candidate section
- reception for the office
- 3 extra handsets to work like extensions

In order to benefit from the benefits of the unlimited SIM mobile package (mobile provider) and the unlimited local and national call package (SIP provider), dial rules will be created so that calls are routed correctly based on the number dialled. The rules will be:-

- calls to mobile numbers routed to use the SIM in the B315
- calls to local, national and non-geographical numbers will be routed to use the SIP provider
- incoming calls for management committee members will be forwarded to their extensions (based on callers' key press) which will automatically dial the relevant member's business number.

Adding extensions and users to the PBX

When the PBX is installed, extension 701 is created by default. However, the committee wants the extensions to be from 801 to 803, leaving extension 701 alone as the administrator's extension. So, three new user extensions will be created. The extensions will be as follows:-

- Anne - extension 801
- Susan - extension 802
- Reception - extension 803

As extension 801 and 802 are not really going to be used, they can be set up as virtual extensions. But the committee wants them to be configured as normal extensions just in case. There is a thought that these extensions can be softphones installed on a couple of laptops and potentially usable when Anne and Susan are working in the project office.

To add extensions

Log into the PBX at http://192.168.2.171, once logged into "Server Management ", go to "Applications" and click on "Extensions".

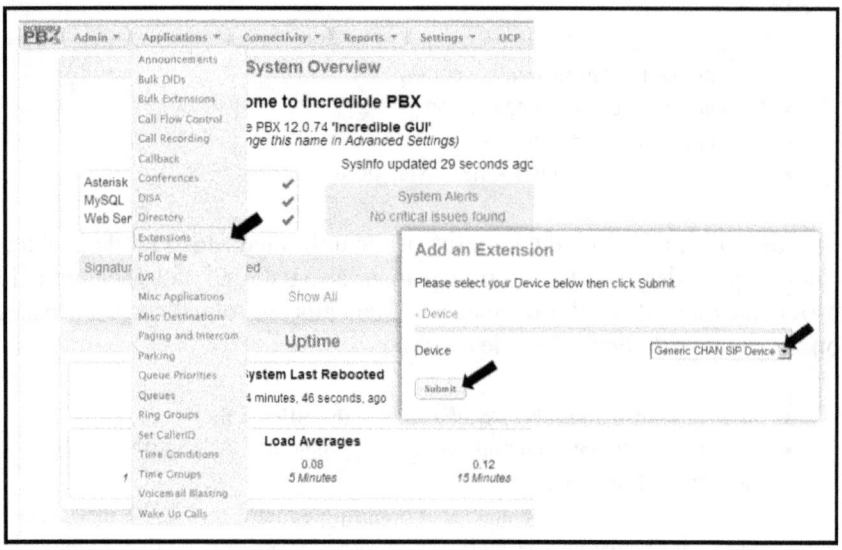

Choose the default "Generic CHAN SIP Device" and click "Submit".

To create an extension for Susan who will be using extension 802, the details will be entered as shown below:-

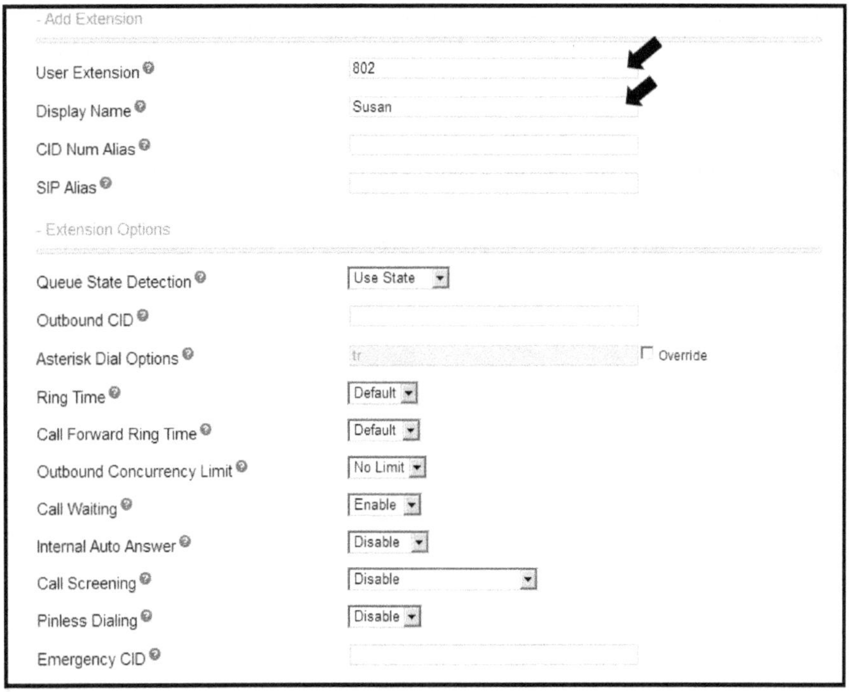

Add Extension	
User Extension	802
Display Name	Susan
CID Num Alias	
SIP Alias	
- Extension Options	
Queue State Detection	Use State
Outbound CID	
Asterisk Dial Options	tr ☐ Override
Ring Time	Default
Call Forward Ring Time	Default
Outbound Concurrency Limit	No Limit
Call Waiting	Enable
Internal Auto Answer	Disable
Call Screening	Disable
Pinless Dialing	Disable
Emergency CID	

A strong password is generated by default, this password will be used to register the extension to the PBX.

| Secret | 162e0b3fcc2442c11872f4fa1b47d065 |

Password (secret) configured for the device. Should be alphanumeric with at least 2 letters and numbers to keep secure. [secret]

The password can be changed to something more memorable, but the recommendation is that it must be strong i.e. includes at least two or more letters and numbers. * In order to register any extensions to the PBX, the username (the extension number e.g. 802) and the "Secret"(password of that extension as shown above) will be used.

The next stage is to enable voicemail so that callers can leave voice messages as email attachments which will be delivered to her mailbox.

Settings are shown below:-

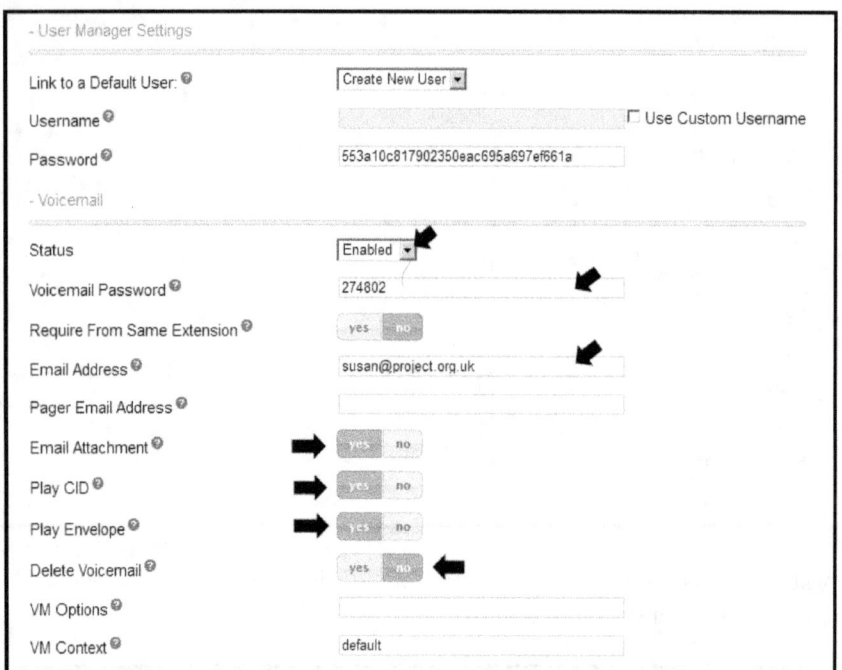

The "Voicemail Password" should be numeric only, since voicemail retrieval can be made from a SIP device like a SIP phone. Make sure that the "Email Address" is entered correctly and that "Email Attachment", "Play CID" and "Play Envelope" are all set to "yes". "Delete Voicemail" is set to "no" to begin with in order to test the reliability of the outgoing email service. If set to "yes", all voice messages will be deleted after they have been sent as emails.

The "Optional Destinations" for "Not Reachable" must be set for "Unvail Voicemail if Enabled" as shown below:-

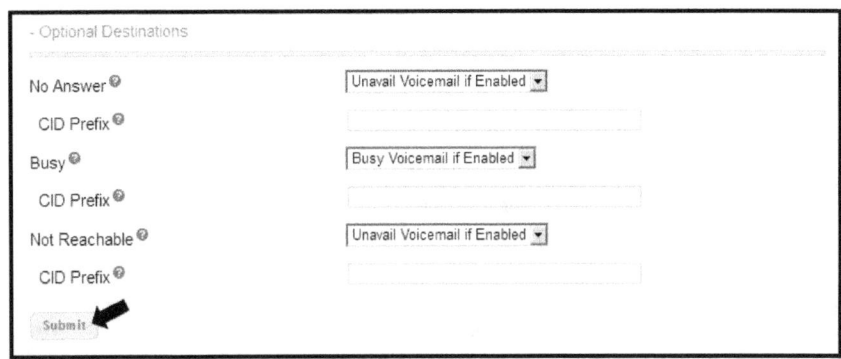

Click "Submit" to save the settings and click "Apply Config" to apply the settings. Remember "Apply Config" must be clicked for any configuration to take effect. From now on, it is assumed that "Apply Config" will be applied for all changes.

Follow Me settings

Since Susan's extension (802) is not a physical device and the main objective at the beginning is for the PBX is forward all calls to her or to send her voicemails, it is necessary to configure "Follow Me" for her extension.

If a caller wants to speak to her by pressing "Option 2" at the "Voice Menu", the PBX will transfer the caller to extension 802, as extension 802 is not registered with PBX i.e. off line. The call will have to be forwarded to Susan..

The PBX will use the "Follow Me" settings to make the external call to her business number. The settings are shown below:-

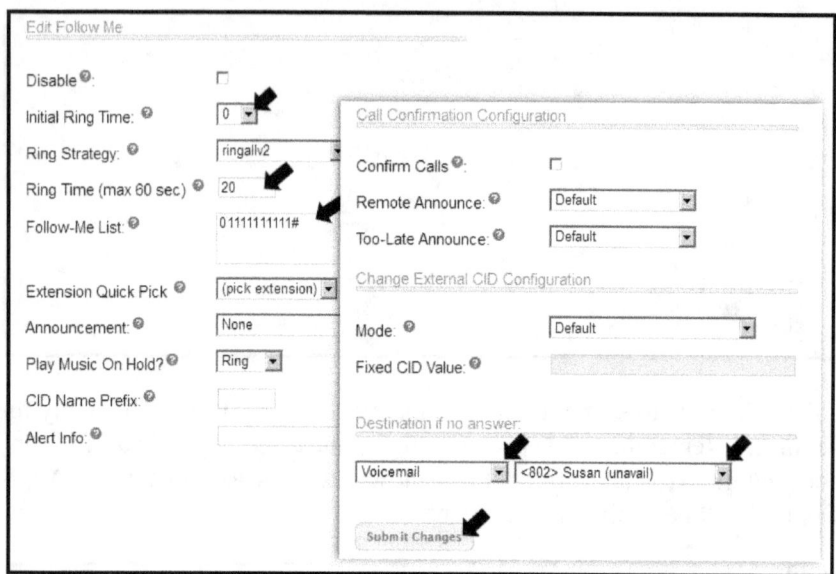

As there will be no physical SIP Device to ring, the "Initial Ring Time" is set to 0, there is no point wasting time trying to ring an extension that does not exist. "Ring Time" for calling Susan's business number is set for 20 seconds. It is possible to enter more than one number to the "Follow-Me-List" and the number should end with the symbol "#". "Destination if no answer" is set to "Voicemail" for extension "802". Since voicemail of extension 802 is set to sending the recorded voice message to Susan's inbox, she will receive the voicemail as an attachment with all details.

It is important to set the "Ring Time" to less than Susan's own business line's "Ring Time", otherwise, her own answer phone will kick in first. Click "Submit Changes" to save the settings and "Apply Config" to complete.

There are also optional settings for "Announcement" i.e. a message saying "your call is being transferred" as well as "Music on Hold". The committee has decided that it is not necessary, but it can be changed later.

Extension creation email

Once the extension is created, Susan receives an email in her inbox to confirm extension details shown below:-

```
Hi ,

Congratulations! Your Incredible PBX account has been created!
You can now use the credentials below:

Username: 802
Password: 553a10c817902350eac695a697ef661a

To login to the following services:

User Control Panel: http://192.168.2.171/ucp


Thanks,
The Incredible PBX Team
```

As the user password generated is extremely difficult to remember, the email is saved in text format so it can be copied and pasted if required again.

*This password is needed to log into the "User Control Panel".

The same process is repeated to create Anne's extension 801. So by now, there are 3 extensions created, 701, 801 and 802.

X-Lite

For testing purposes, X-Lite (softphone) is used to create the 2 SIP devices to act as the extensions. The idea is that, if necessary, headsets can be used and these two extensions can act as real SIP phones. However, at this stage, they will only be used for testing and will not be running once testing is completed. X-Lite is downloaded at:-

http://www.counterpath.com/x-lite-download/

Once downloaded, it is installed on two of the laptops to create the two extensions. Once the X-Lite Softphone software is loaded, go to "Softphone" and click on "Account Settings", enter settings as follows:-

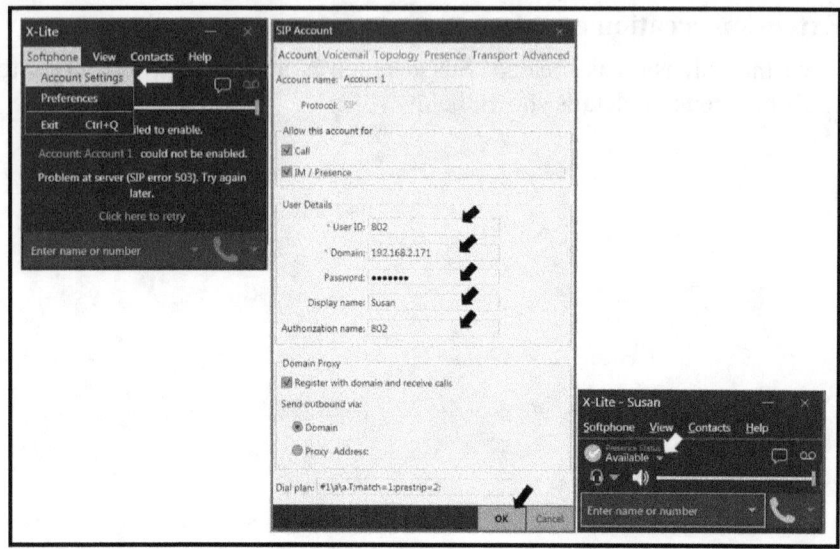

Once all the relevant details are entered, the device is registered on the PBX and the "Presence Status" changes to "Available". Repeat the same process for extension 801 on the other laptop.

By dialing extension 701 with X-Lite from each laptop, the voicemail message of 701 is played; this confirms that the extensions are working. At this stage, the extensions cannot make any outside calls, so "Follow Me" cannot be tested.

Configuring the Gigaset A580 IP

Reception extension 803 is the Gigaset A580IP, the process of creating the extension is the same as the 801 and 802. Except for this extension, there is no need to configure the "Follow Me" settings. Once the extension has been created, the A580 will need to be configured to register to with PBX.

The IP address of A580 has been set to 192.168.2.198 when it was used at George's home. Since it is within the same network of the B315, there is no need to change its network settings. As with other devices, it can be accessed for configurations via its web interface. Type in 192.168.2.198 from a browser and the log in screen appear as below:-

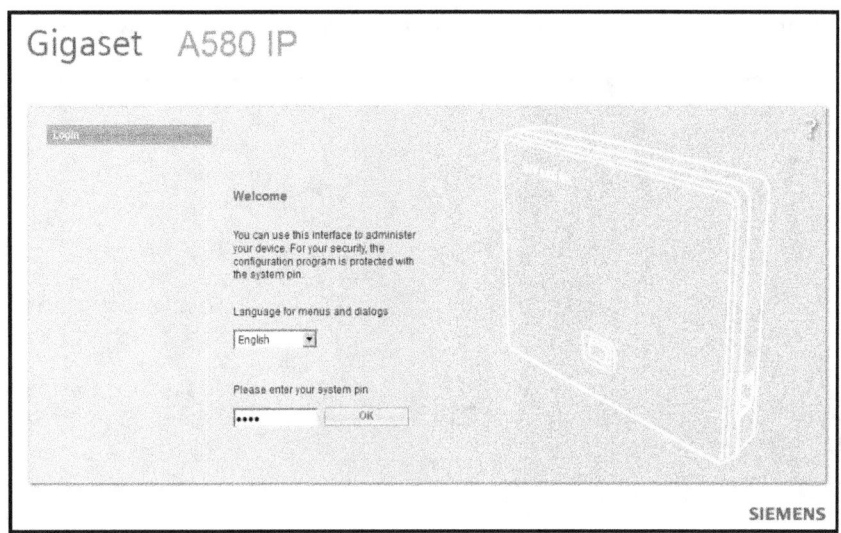

The default "system pin" of "0000" is used to log in. This "system pin" should be changed later to a random set of 4 numbers to make it more secured. Once logged in, choose "Settings" and click "IP Configuration".

Change the settings to match the network requirements as shown below:-

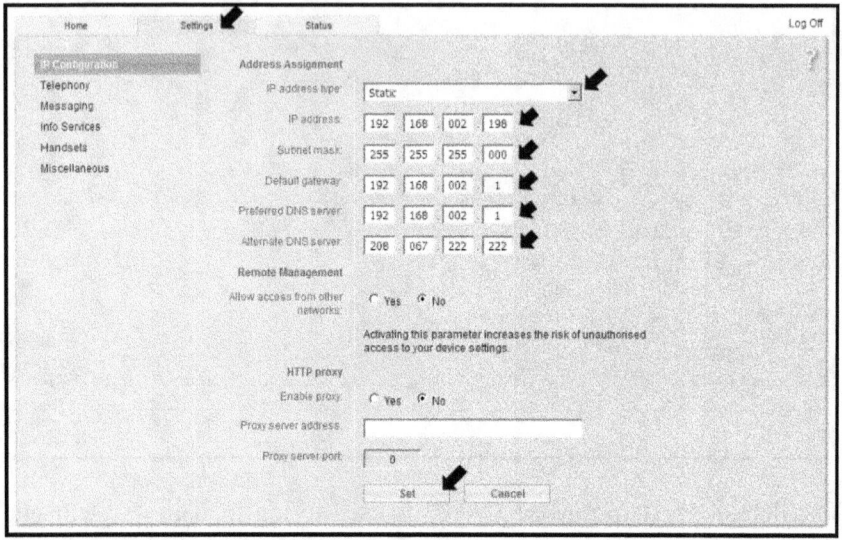

The "Alternative DNS Server" can be any valid DNS server on the internet. Complete this stage by clicking "Set".

Next, click "Telephony" then "Connections" and click the "Edit" button. The settings for this connection is now displayed, enter details as shown below:-

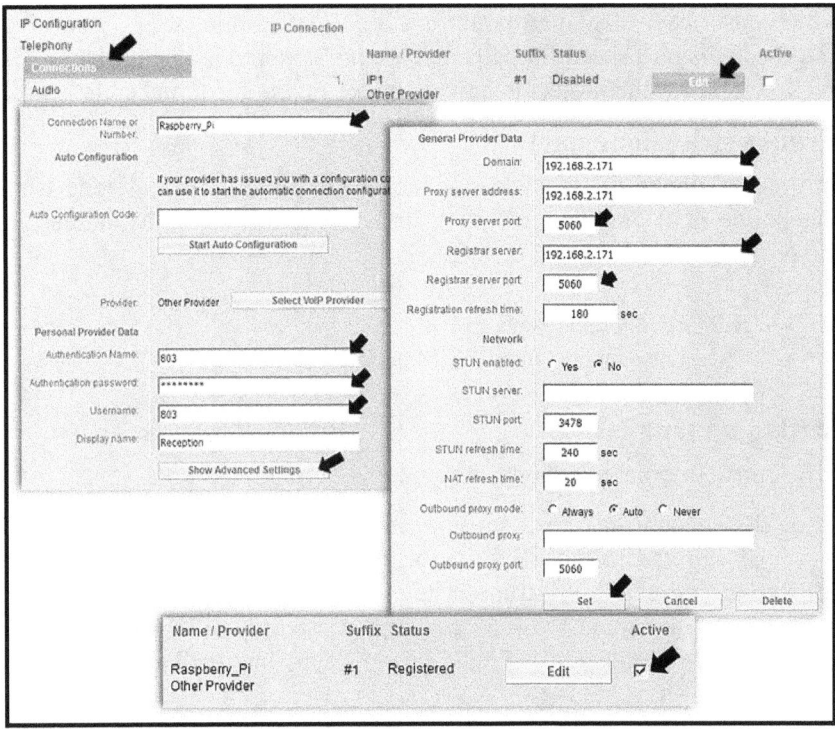

The "Authentication Name" is just the extension number and the "Authentication password" is the "Secret" that is generated when the extension is created.

Click "Set" to complete this stage of the configuration. Once the screen returns to the "Connections" screen, tick the "Active" checkbox and the "Status" now shows "Registered".

The reception extension is now set and the A580 is ready to make and receive internal calls. A test call to extension 701 reaches the voicemail announcement. A test call from extension 801 with a headset allows for a full good quality conversation.

Outgoing calls

After careful research, the committee agrees to use Soho66, a local SIP provider and has subscribed to their multi user VOIP package which costs £5 + VAT per month. The "Unlimited UK Landline Calls" package which costs £8 + VAT per month is added. An additional £20 + VAT of call credits is purchased for calls that are not covered by the package. The PBX system for the project is now ready for making external calls.

Trunks (telephone line)

In order to make calls outside of the local network, at least one trunk (telephone line) must be created at the PBX and must be available. For the project, two trunks will be created:-

- SIP line (internet telephony)
- fixed line using the mobile SIM package

Setting up trunks

SIP Trunk (Internet telephony - provider is Soho66)

Once the account has been set up with a prepaid call package and £20 worth of call credit, the PBX can be registered with the SIP provider's SIP server to create a SIP trunk. The provider has provided details of the account as username: 1234567 and the password is 7654321, the SIP server is sip.soho66.co.uk. Trunk set up detail instructions supplied by SOHO66 are show below:-

```
Outbound Caller ID: 01911111111
Trunk Name: Soho66
PEER Details:
 type=friend
 insecure=very
 nat=yes
 qualify=no   ; this is important!!
 canreinvite=no
 authuser=1234567 [account name supplied by provider]
 username=1234567 [account name supplied by provider]
 fromuser=1234567 [account name supplied by provider]
 fromdomain=sip.soho66.co.uk [sip server of Soho66]
 secret=7654321 [account password supplied by provider]
 host=sip.soho66.co.uk [sip server of Soho66]
 dtmfmode=rfc2833
 context=from-trunk
 disallow=all
 allow=alaw&ulaw&gsm
 port=8060
USER Context: from-trunk
USER Details: fromdomain=sip.soho66.co.uk
Register String: 1234567: 7654321@sip.soho66.co.uk/ 1234567
```

To set up a trunk on the PBX, log into the PBX at http://192.168.2.171 again, go to "Connectivity" and Click on "Trunks" as shown below:-

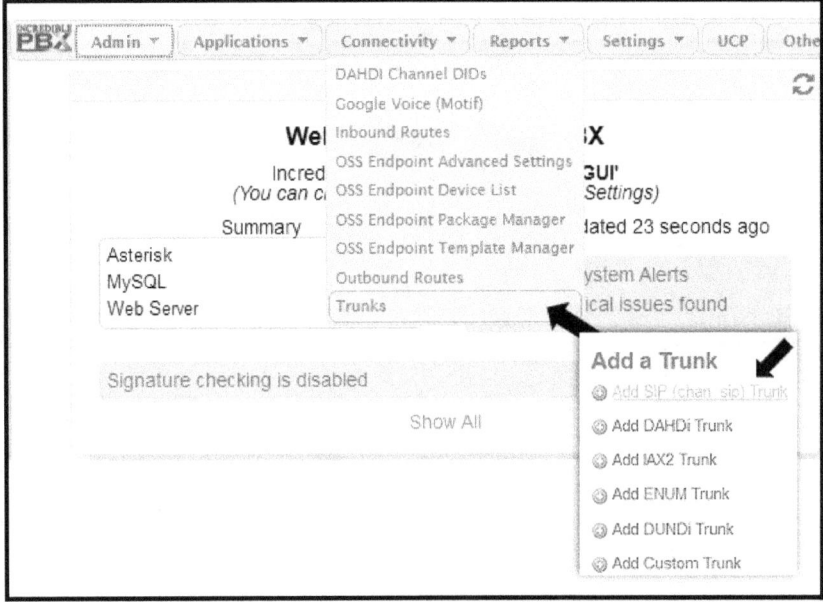

Click "Add SIP (chan_sip) Trunk" next.

The trunk configuration screen is displayed, enter "Trunk Name" and the "Outbound CallerID" and the "Maximum Channels" as shown below:-

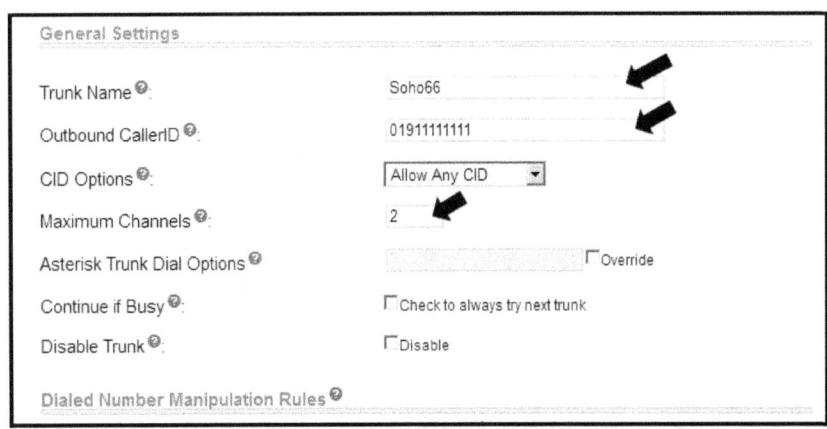

Next enter settings as supplied by the SIP provider as shown below:-

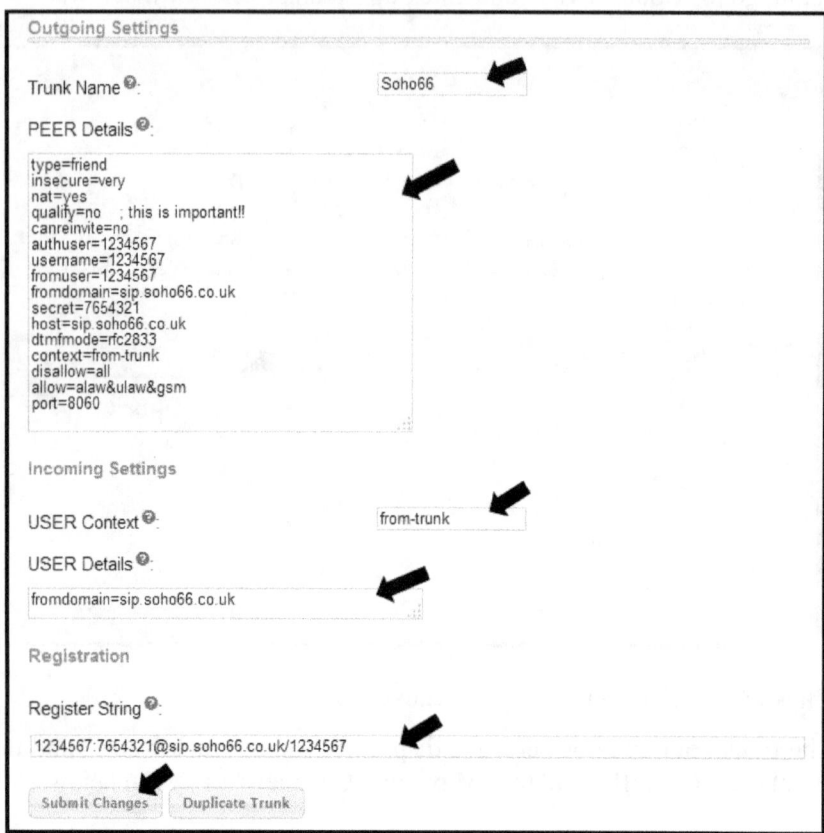

Click "Submit Changes" and "Apply Config" to apply settings. Now that there is a telephone line (actually 2) as set by the "Maximum Channels" above, an outbound rule is required. This rule will allow extensions to make calls based on the numbers dialled. To create an "Outbound Route", go to "Connectivity" again and choose "Outbound Routes".

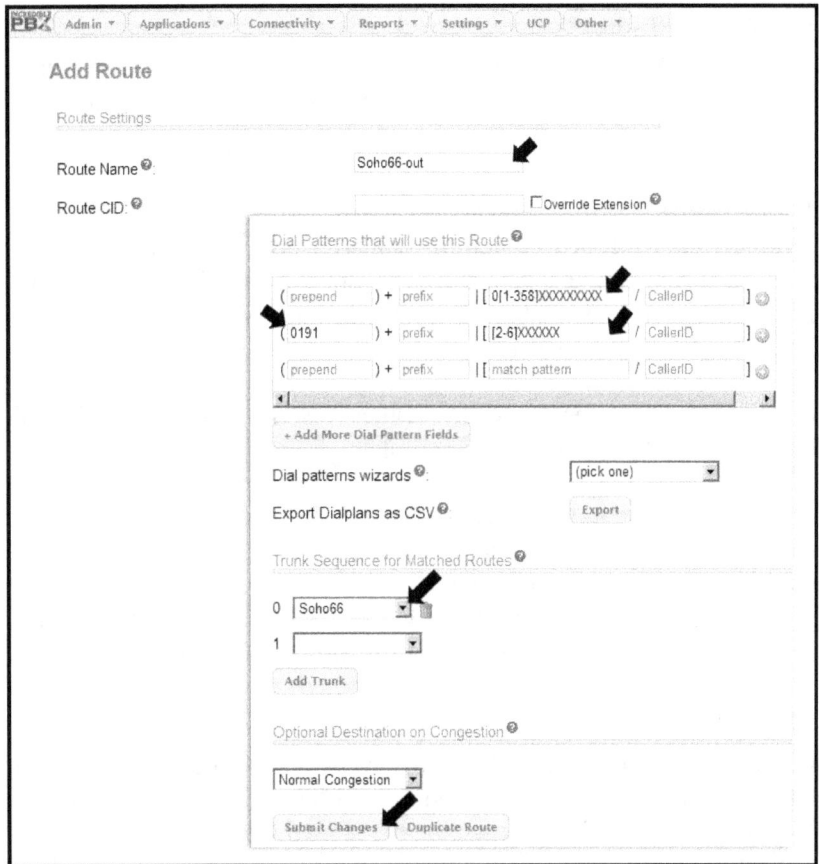

Give the route a name as shown above. The next stage is to create "Dial Patterns" or rules for extensions to use this route by matching the numbers dialled.

To cover all likely telephone numbers that may be called by staff of the project, two patterns are set as shown above.

For national numbers

0[1-358]XXXXXXXXX - the number 0 is dialled, followed by a number between 1 and 3 or the number 5 or the number 8 and followed by exactly nine numbers.

For local numbers

[2-6]XXXXXX - if the first number dialled is between 2 and 6 and followed by six numbers, then add 0191 first when dialling this number. This saves the caller from having to dial the local STD code first as is required by the SIP provider.

"Trunk Sequence For Matched Routes" is set for "Soho66". Click "Submit" and "Apply Config" to complete.

The above configuration means that all local and national numbers dialled will be using the "Soho66" trunk. The settings do not allow for international or premium rate number calls. Mobile calls are not included also because they should be made via the SIM package. One local and one national call is made, both calls work with good quality.

Mobile Trunk

In order to make calls to mobiles, the A580 needs to use the SIM in the B315 to benefit from the unlimited calls offered by the mobile provider. Effectively, the mobile trunk will be the "Fixed Line" (PSTN) at the back of the B315. There are two ways of initiating a call by using the "Fixed Line" of the B315. By default, if a number is dialled and the green dial button is held for a couple seconds, the call will be made using the fixed line.

Although holding the dial button will work, the committee wants the process to be simple. After all, if the caller forgets to hold the dial button, the call will result in failure. The alternative is to create a dial rule for mobile calls with the A580.

Log in to the web interface of the A580 at http://192.168.2.198.

Go to "Settings" then "Telephony" and "Dialling Plans". Enter the settings for the "Dialing Plan" and click the "Active" check box to activate the settings as shown below:-

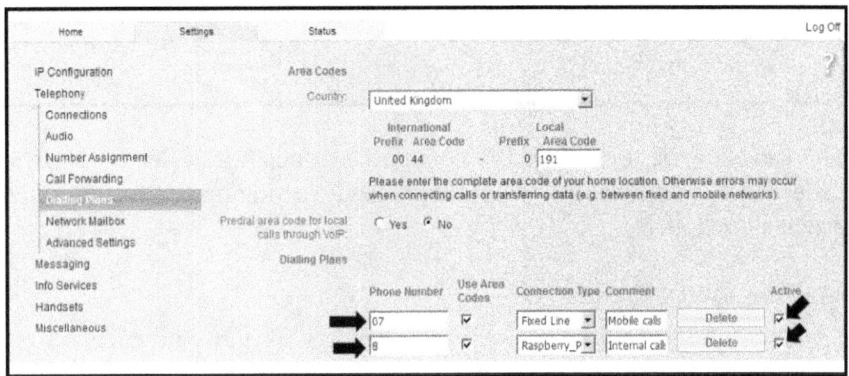

The settings mean the A580 will use the "Fixed Line" of the B315 whenever the number dialed begins with 07. Calls between extensions 803, 801 and 802 are covered by the second rule which allows numbers beginning with 8 to use the "Pi". Now any handset will be able to make calls by just dialing the required number. A quick test to one of the staff's mobile confirms that the "Dialing Plan" is working correctly.

*Although the PBX is not able to dial emergency 999 as there is no "Dialing Plan" for this number , it is possible to use the mobile connection to do so by holding the dial button for a couple of seconds after dialing. The committee members decide that as all the staff have their own mobile phones anyway, it is not really that important.

Configuring the handsets

The A580 has its own way of transferring calls as it is basically a closed system. The handsets need to be configured as if they are extensions. Go to "Settings" and "Handsets", enter the setting as shown below:-

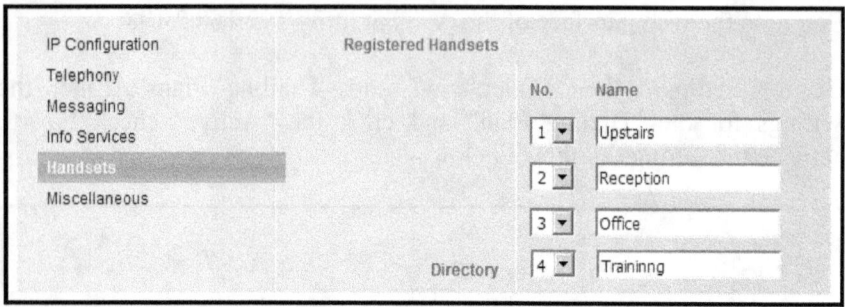

The handsets are named by the committee to make it easier for staff to understand by using the room name and section names rather than extension numbers.

Making internal calls

Since the A580 system treats every handset as the equivalent of an extension; internal calls to other handsets will be the same as dialling another extension. To make an internal call, press the "INT" button on the bottom right as shown below:-

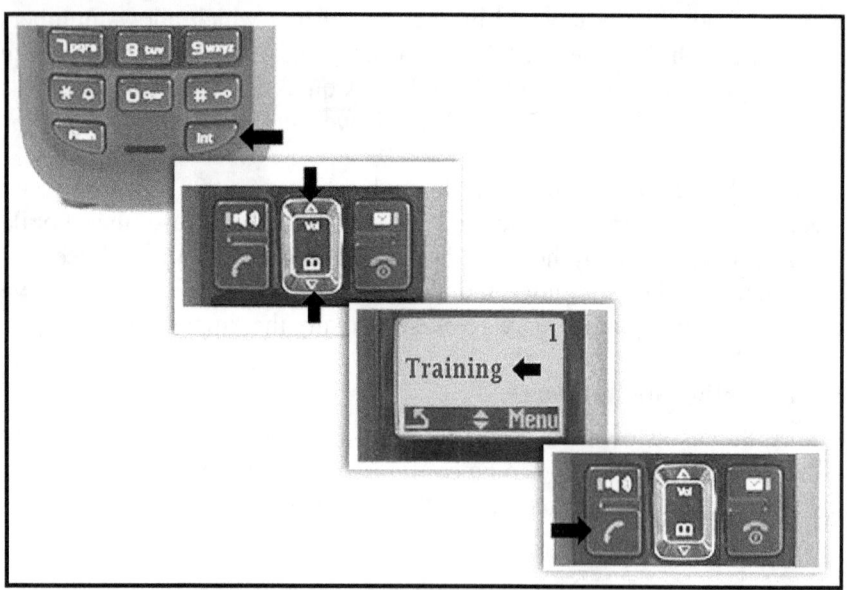

By using the up and down button, choose the handset to call e.g. Training. Once the correct handset (Training) appears, press the green dial button to make call.

All the handsets are now ready to make external and internal calls by following the instructions shown before.

Incoming calls

Since the committee has decided to use an IVR (interactive voice response) system with background music to deal with all incoming calls, the first thing that must be done is to create these voice prompts. The required prompts are as follows:-

- during office hours "IVR" welcome message giving callers the three options*
- after hours welcome message giving callers option to go to voicemail
- voicemail greetings for Anne
- voicemail greetings for Susan
- voicemail greetings for reception

*Options to call Susan, Anne or Reception.

Interactive Voice response

The project decides to create all the voiceovers and use copyright free music for their PBX system. The management committee thinks the project will sound much more professional this way.

There are loads of music available for use with the VOIP PBXs, some are free and some not. There are professionally created music specifically designed for on hold music at a price to suit any requirements. They also come in different formats e.g. MP3, WAV etc. Some sites that are worth having a look at are:-

- http://www.onhold2go.co.uk
- http://www.classiccat.net

https://kamazoy.uk/royalty-free-completely-free-hold-music-mp3-downloads/.

Although a lot of the music is free, it is worth checking with the sites first, the last thing the project wants is to be accused of using copyrighted materials without permission.

Audacity

There are many ways to add voiceovers to on hold music including using a headset plugged into the audio ports of the PC or using a smart phone to record and download to a PC for mixing. A freely available open-source software called Audacity can be downloaded from the link –

http://audacity.sourceforge.net/

The Audacity software is relatively easy to use, very powerful and it is free. Once the software is downloaded, run the installation program and complete the installation just like any other downloaded programs. Copy the background music to a folder in the file system e.g. Track, to make it available to Audacity.

Creating the welcome message with background music

Before creating the voice message, background "welcome" music needs to be generated. George downloaded several suitable tracks from one of the websites offering "free to use" on hold music.

Using open-source (Audacity) software to create the projects own on hold music. The music chosen to be used as background music for the welcome message is loaded into Audacity by opening it as shown below:-

It is always best to work with the highest possible quality first, so the sampling rates etc. is left at the highest current quality (16 bit at 44KHz) for the time being. Since the audio format required by the PBX is 8KHz mono, the music needs to be converted to mono first.

The current format of the music downloaded is 16 bit stereo quality, in order to make it mono, one of the music tracks must be removed.

Run Audacity, go to "File" and "Open" by clicking the file"01 Track 1.mp3". Now click "01 Track 1" to choose it and then "Split Stereo to Mono". One of the tracks can now be removed by clicking the "x" as show below. Listen to the single track that is left and listen to the quality of the remaining track.

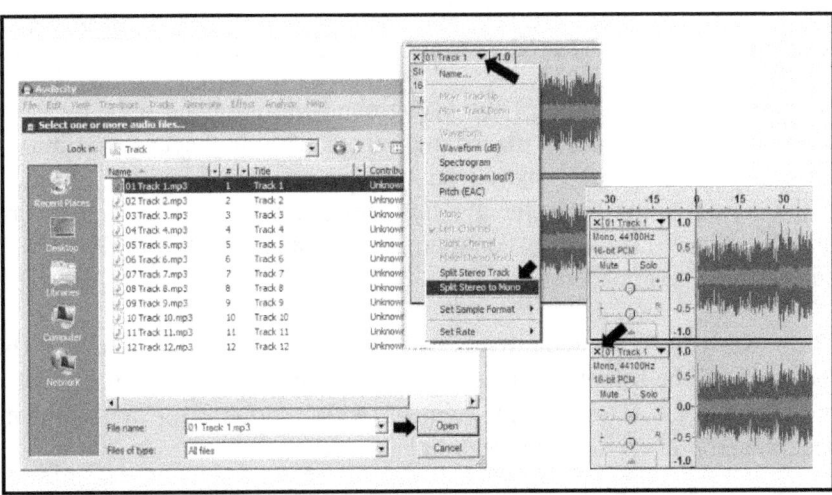

Despite the fact that one of the tracks is removed, the sound quality still seems quite good. Remember it is still 16 bit quality; it will probably lose some quality later.

The volume level of the music can be adjusted by using the envelope tool. By click on the appropriate position to add a point, the volume of the music can be adjusted at the specified point. The diagram below shows an increase in volume towards 35 seconds.

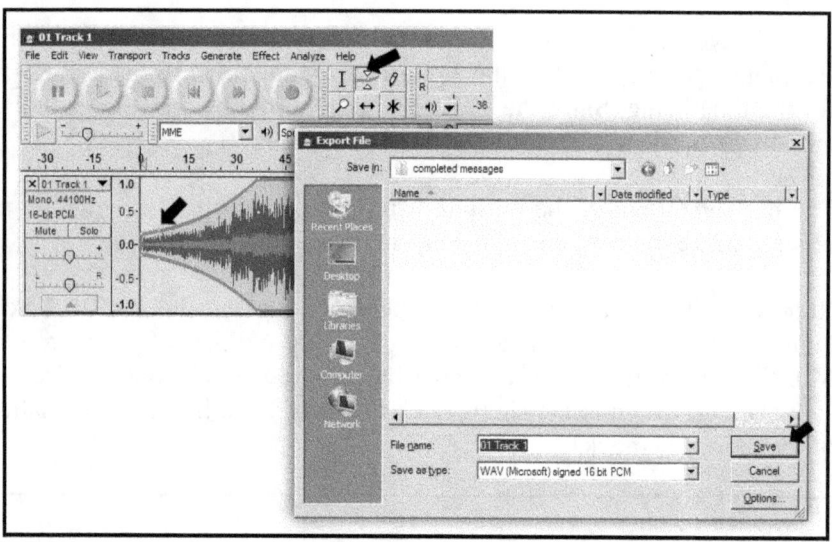

By adjusting the volume of the background music at the right location, the voice message can be placed and mixed with the background music. Make sure the volume of background music is set to a low enough level at the correct point where the greeting message and voice prompt will be inserted. Once this stage is completed, it can be saved to the file system and ready to be reloaded again.

The next stage is to record the voice greeting and voice prompt. The message will be something like "Thank you for calling our project office, in order ....press 1 for the employment section, press 2 for the candidate section and press 3 for our reception."

Audacity itself can be used to record the message and the prompts. By plugging a good quality microphone into the microphone socket of the computer, Audacity can be used for voice recording. Record by choosing "Microsoft Sound Mapper - Input" and clicking the "Record" button to start.

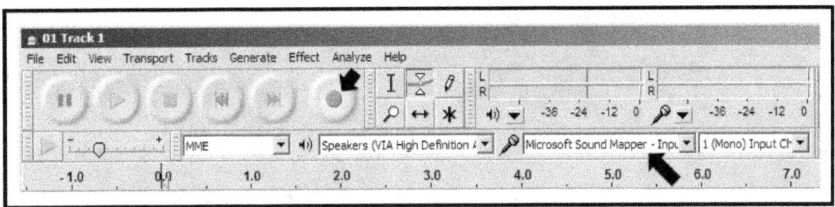

A good quality voice recording is achieved by trial and error. Recorded in 16 bit to get the best quality to begin with, however, it is unlikely to remain as good when the audio is downgraded to the format required by the PBX. Once the voice recording is completed save it to the file system.

Load up the saved background music file (e.g. 01 Track 1.wav) by clicking "File" and "Open", once it is opened, go to "File" and click "Import" and choose the voice message previously recorded and saved.

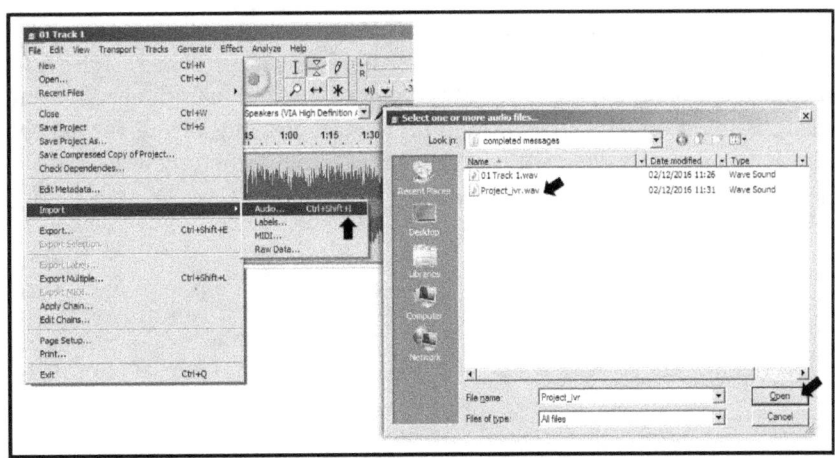

Once the file is imported, use the "Selection tool" to highlight the whole of the "Voice message track" above to select the whole track.

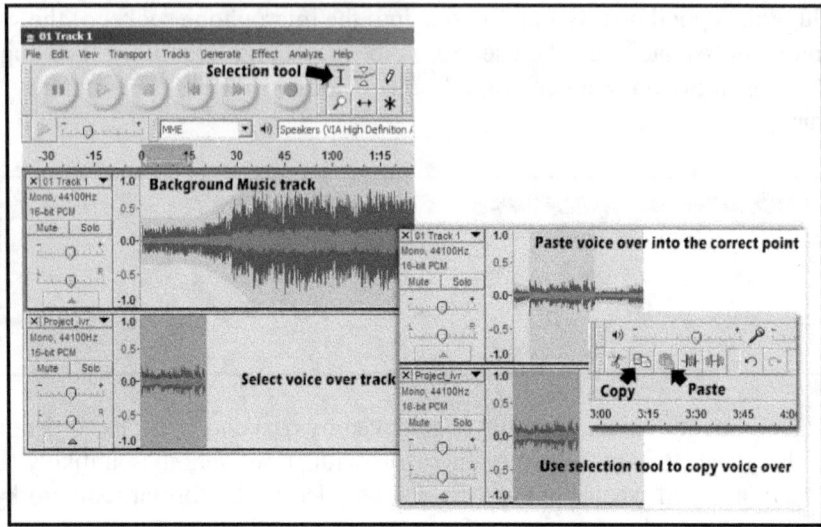

Then click "Copy" and paste the selected sound track into the relevant location of the background music track above it.

Make sure the "Voice message" sound track is removed by clicking the "x", leaving only the mixed voice and music sound track. Listen to the track and make sure the quality of the voice message over the background music is good enough. It is now time to save the music in a format that the PBX can use. It does not matter what original format the tracks are in, they need to be "16bit 8KHz wave" with a suffix of .wav for the PBX to use.

Choose "Edit" from the top and click on "Preference..." to open the "Preference" settings window.

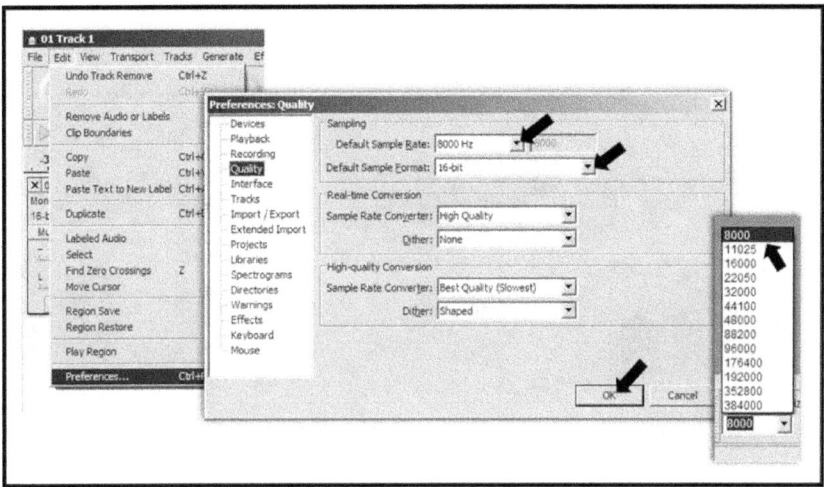

Set "Quality" to 8KHz, 16-bit as shown below. At the bottom left of the screen, set project rate to 8KHz as below.

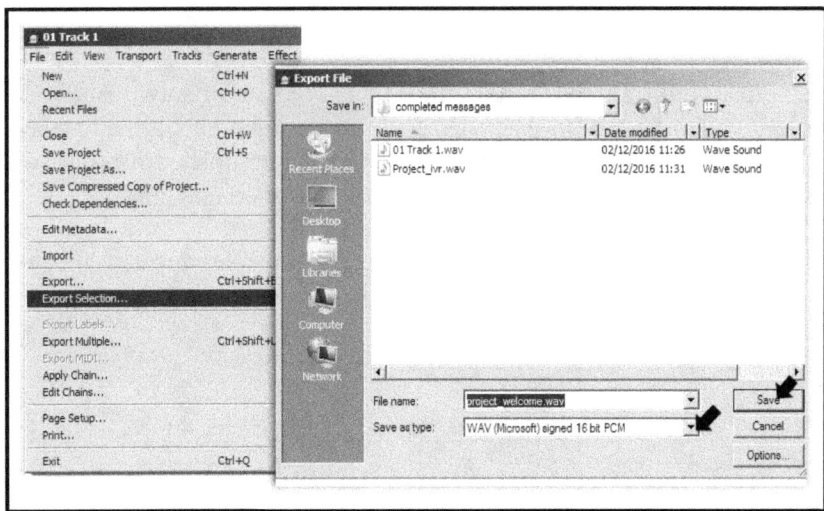

Once the format is set, the sound track needs to be exported as one file. By using the "Selection Tool", highlight the part of the track to be exported. Go to "File" and choose "Export selection". If the whole track is needed, just choose "Export". Make sure the file is exported as 16 bit .wav format. Edit the "Metadata" if desired and click "OK" to save the file.

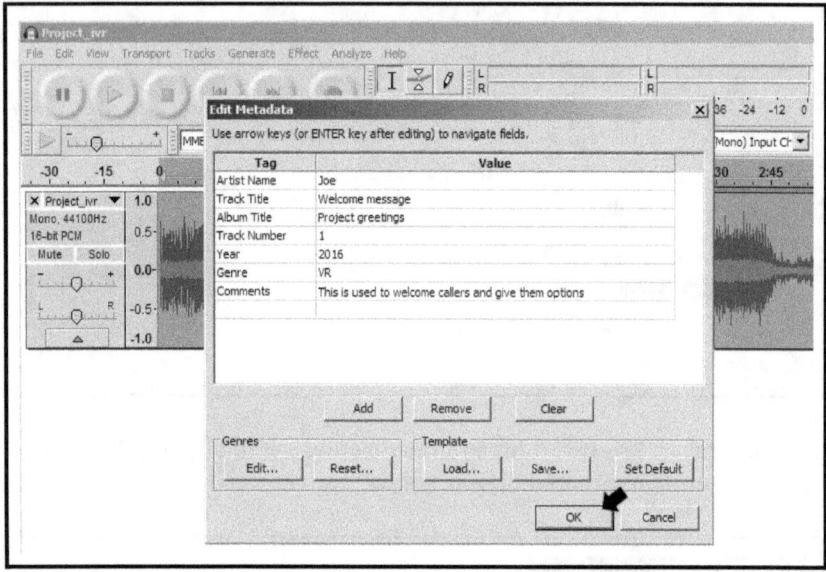

Just to confirm that the file is saved correctly, open file project_welcome.wav in Audacity again, the format should be displayed on the left hand side of the track. Listen to the completed message with background music to confirm that the quality is good enough.

Once all the necessary voice and greetings prompts are created, they will be used for the next stage i.e. by the IVR and voicemail greetings of Anne and Susan.

To upload all the voice prompts, go to "Admin" and click "System Recordings".

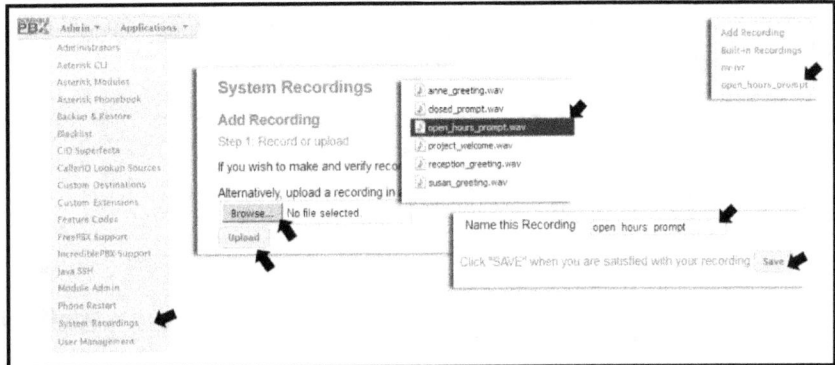

Browse the file system and locate the previously created prompt and click "Upload". The name of the recording appears as the original name of the file, click "save" button to save the prompt. Now the "opening_hours_prompt" appears on the top right list of recordings. Repeat the process for all other prompts.

IVR (Interactive Voice Response) prompts

Once all the "Voice Prompts" are created, the next step is to create two "IVRs", one for "Office hours and the other for "Out of hours". To create an IVR, go to "Applications" and click on "IVR". Click "Add a new IVR" and fill in details as below:-

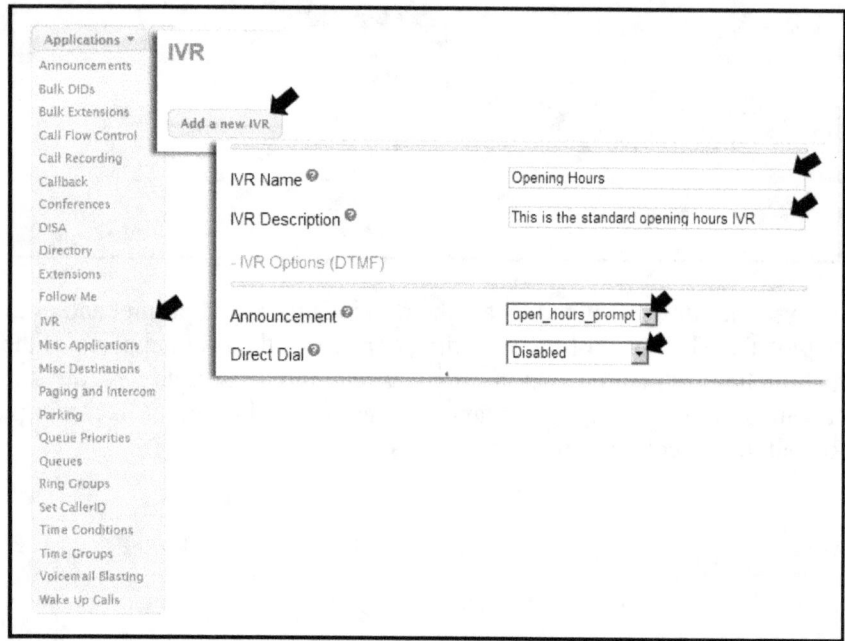

Give the "IVR" a name and choose the relevant voice prompt that was created earlier. To simplify the process, set "Timeout Retries" to 3 and "Invalid Destinations" to extension 803 (Reception).

This means if the caller presses the wrong option three times or do nothing for ten seconds, the call will be forwarded to extension 803. This should cover all options to handle any valid incoming calls during office hours.

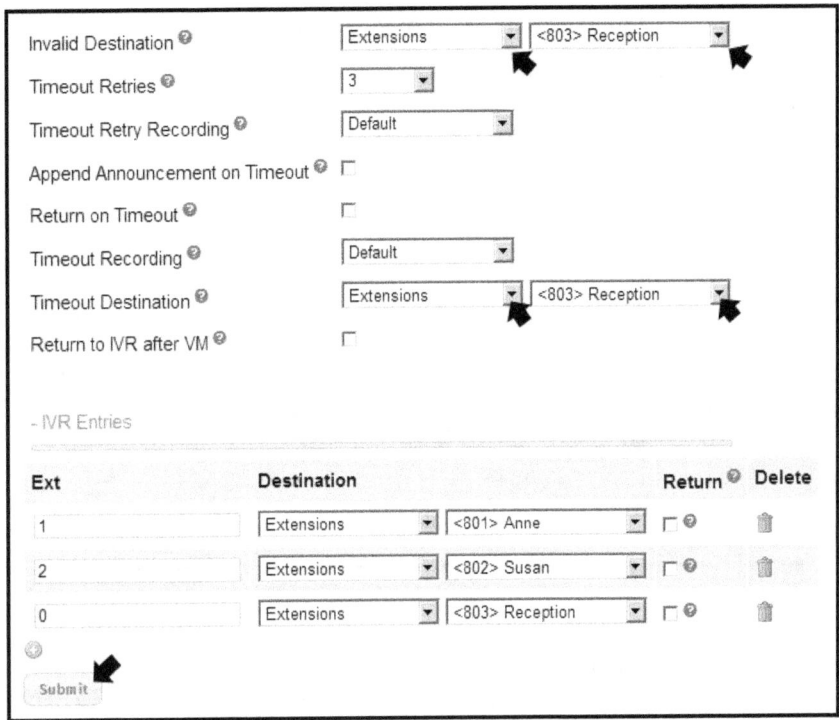

At the "IVR Entries" section, enter the three options that the caller may wish to choose as shown above. Click the "Submit" button and "Activate Config" to complete.

Repeat this process to create the "IVR" for out of office hours. Of course, the "Out Of Hours" "IVR" should play the "closed_prompt". The caller can then either choose to press "0" to leave a voice message or call back again.

The settings for "Out of Hours" is shown below:-

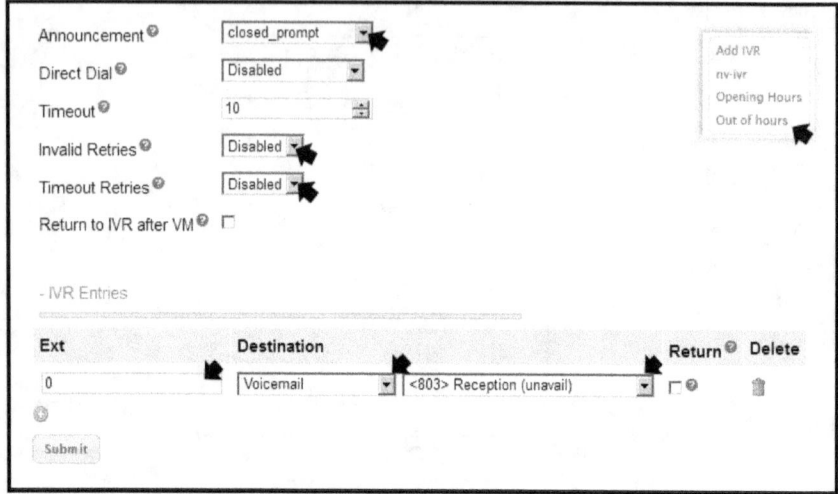

Incoming calls

Since the project operates between Monday and Friday between 9.00am and 5.00pm only, incoming calls outside these hours will have to be answered differently. To achieve this, the system relies on "Timing Conditions" and "Timing Groups". Based on the "Timing Conditions", different "Timing Groups" will be used. To simplify the system, there will only be one "Time Condition" – "Standard" and two "Time Groups" – "Office Hours" and "Out of Hours".

- "Office Hours" is between 9.00am and 5.00pm Monday to Friday
- "Out of Hours" is basically closed and covers all times

There is going to be two "Timing Groups" to deal with incoming calls during office hours and out of hours as described above.

Time group

Two "Time Groups" will be created, one for the normal working week and weekends and one for holidays and holiday weekends. To create an "Opening Hours" "Time Group", go to "Applications" and click on "Time Groups". Fill in all fields as shown below:-

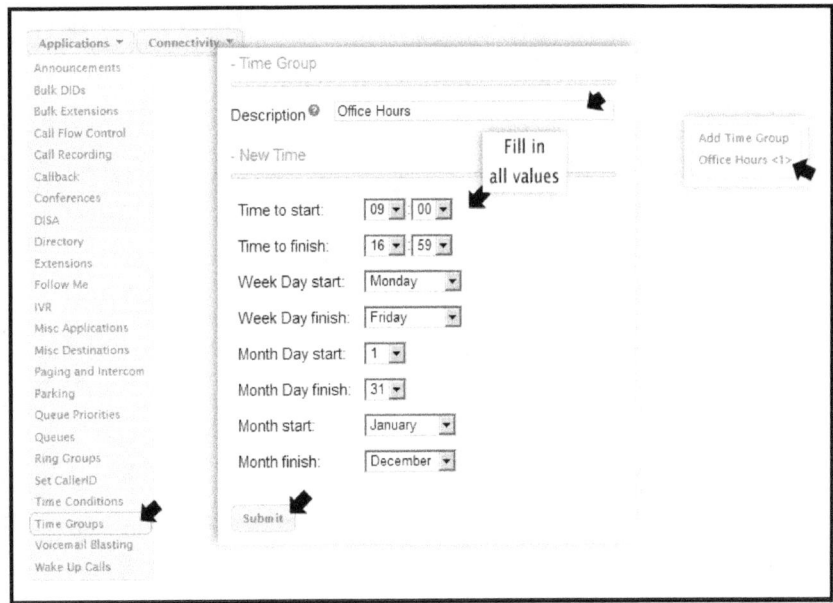

Once all fields are successfully entered, click the "Submit" button and "Apply Config" to complete. A "Time Group" called "Office Hours <1>" will appear at the top right of the "Time Group" screen.

Repeat the same process to create an "Out of Hours" "Time Group". The only difference will be "Time to start" will be 00:00 and "Time to finish" will be 23:59 i.e. closed all the time. This "Time Group" will be used for all holidays and holiday weekends etc.

"Time Condition"

To create a "Time Condition", go to "Applications", click on "Time Conditions". Enter details as below:-

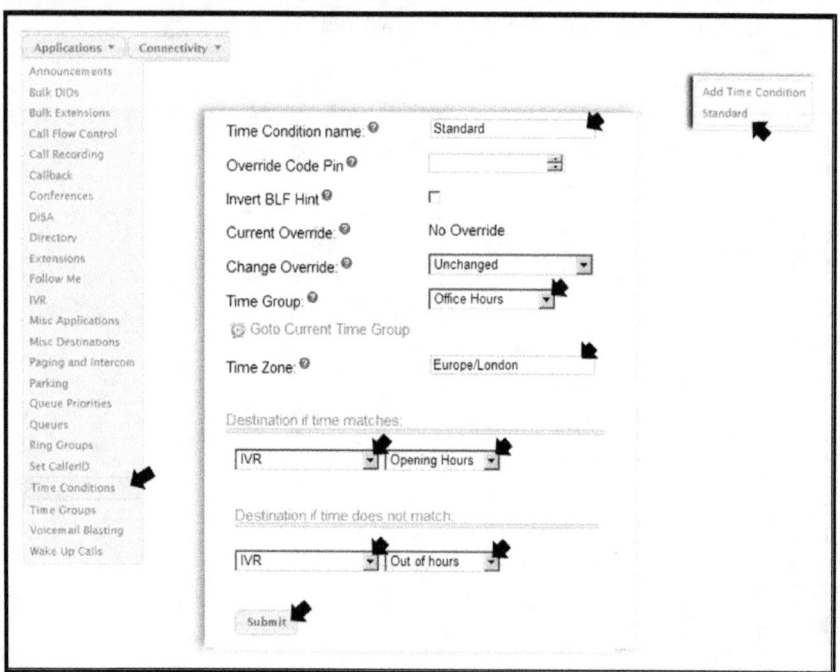

Give the "Time Condition" a name e.g. "Standard". This will be the one and only "Time Condition" for simplicity. Choose the "Time Group" of "Office Hours" and "IVR" destinations as shown above.

Although it is possible to create different "Timing Conditions" and "Time Groups" to cover weekends, bank holidays, Christmas, New Year and Easter, it will be too complex for the staff to manage.

By using just one "Time Condition", the reception staff only has to change the "Time Group" to "Out of Hours" and the "IVRs" to "Out of Hours" the evening before closing for the holiday and then change them back on return.

Time based call flows

The PBX is now configured with "Time Group" "Office Hours" i.e. 09:00 to 17:00 Monday to Friday using the "Opening Hours" "IVR" and the "Out of Hours" "IVR" for when the office is shut.

For holidays and bank holidays etc., the "Out of Hours" "Time Group" and "Out of Hours" "IVR" will be used.

Inbound route

One inbound route is already set when the PBX is created. It is the "Default" route which means all incoming calls will be handled based on this setting. For simplicity, this will be the only route used by the project.

To modify this route, go to "Connectivity" and click "Inbound Routes" and change the settings to below:-

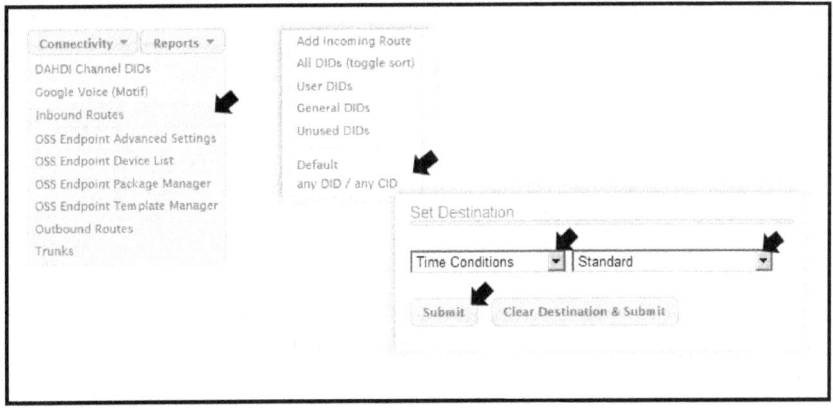

The settings above means all calls will follow the settings of the "Standard" "Time Conditions". Remember to click "Submit" button and "Apply Config" to finish.

Incoming calls during office hours

During office hours, callers will receive a voice prompt ("IVR" "Opening Hours") for the employment section, candidate section and reception. These calls will be dealt with as follows:-

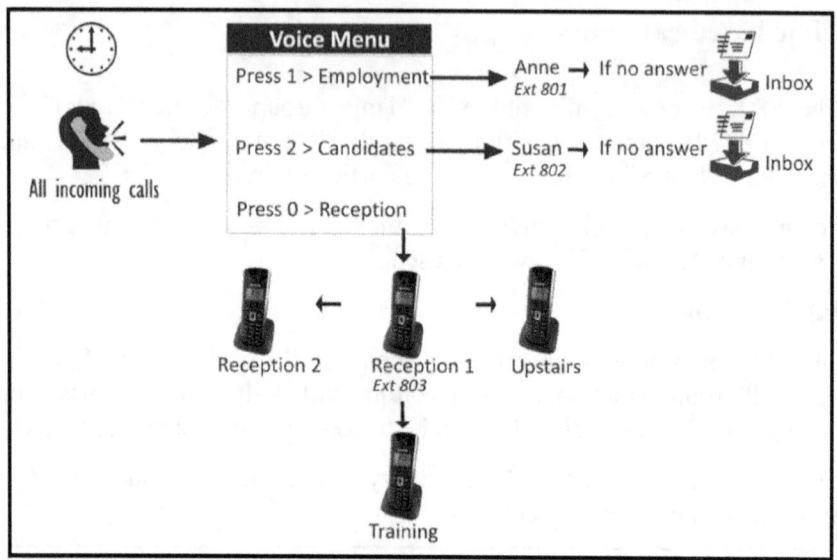

The IVR will answer all calls and play the "opening_hours_prompt" with three options:-

- "press 1 for employment section"
- "press 2 for candidates section"
- "press 0 for reception"

The first two options forward the calls to the business numbers of the committee members via their extension's "Follow-Me" settings. If a call is not answered within a certain number of rings, the call will be sent to voicemail of the relevant committee member. This should allow the two management committee members to directly handle a lot of the enquiries.

Option to press 0 for reception will ring at the receptionist's handset, from the handset, the receptionist can transfer that call internally to the relevant handset based on its location e.g. "Training" as suggested by one member.

Receiving an external call and transferring it

The process is as follows:-

- reception handset rings
- receptionist answers call
- press right display key "Menu" to bring up choices
- press up and down arrow keys to find "Internal"
- press right display key "OK" to choose internal transfer
- press up and down to find "Training"
- press green talk button to call "Training"
- once "Training" accepts call, press red end call button

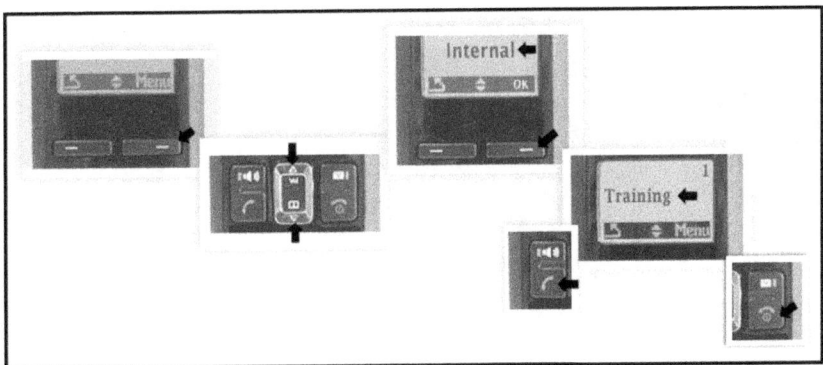

The three options should cover all requirements for any incoming calls. However, there will be occasions when further actions will be necessary. One such situation is if a caller presses 0 to speak to the receptionists but she really needs to speak to the management committee member dealing with candidates.

Under such circumstances, the receptionist can either take a message and then contact the committee member later or transfer the call externally. In order to transfer the call externally, the receptionist must use the "external dial" function of the handset to dial the extension of the committee member.

The process of transferring a call to an external number is similar to transferring to an internal handset. The only difference is the receptionist chooses "External" instead of "Internal" and dials the business number of Susan or extension 802 to transfer the call.

Although this function should work, the committee has decided that it may be too complex for the system to work reliably and decides that it should only be used if the call is urgent.

Out of hours calls for a normal week

The "Standard" "Time Conditions" is configured to answer all calls during working hours as describe above. Outside these hours, the "IVR" will play the "out_of_hours" prompt and the caller can only dial 0 to leave a voice message or call back.

Incoming calls after office hours

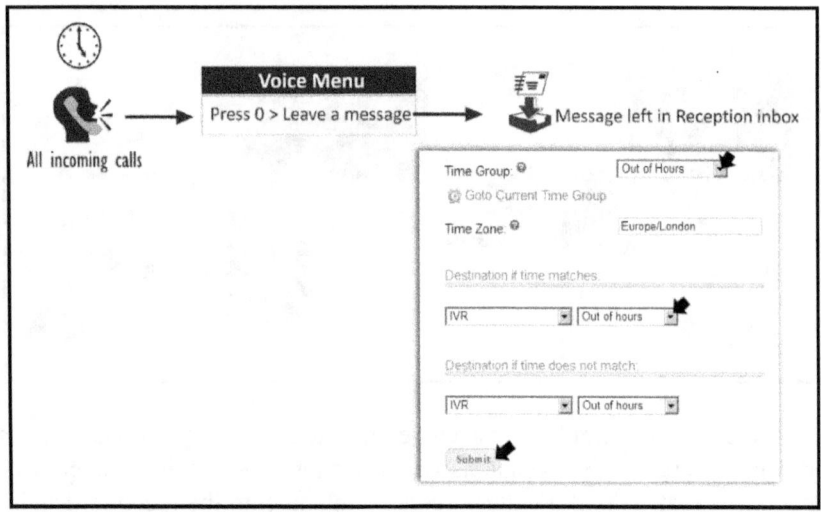

When a caller presses 0, the call will be forwarded to the reception voicemail.

For holiday weekends, Christmas and Easter holidays, this process will operate. The process can be set by changing the "Time Conditions". The "Time Group" needs to be changed to "Closed" and the "IVRs" need to be changed to "Out of Hours" as well.

As stated earlier, this process must be activated the evening before the holidays start and changed back on the morning the project office opens again.

Once the incoming calls for both during and after office hours have been set up, several incoming calls are made at different hours to test the system. The results confirm that the system is working exactly as it should and the system is successfully implemented.

Conclusion

The Raspberry Pi has been used by numerous organisations for numerous projects. Despite the fact that it is originally designed for the education market, its power and flexibility has enabled it to be used for many commercial applications, in particular, as in the embedded device market.

The reasons for using a Raspberry Pi as a PBX in a real life situation have been explained by this book. It's powerful and advance hardware together with the proven reliability and functionality of Incredible PBX™ makes it a realistic competitor in the IPPBX device market.

The book also shows some of the weaknesses of setting up such a system, in particular, the process of installation and configuration seems incomplete as well as a bit confusing.

The installation and set up process can be completed within a few minutes, unfortunately, the default settings do not work well in the UK. For example, leaving the "Time zone /country" settings at the beginning at default (thinking it can easily be changed later) will lead to timing issues with voicemails etc.

By using this book as a guide, it is possible for the "IT literate" reader to set up a Raspberry Pi as a VOIP PBX and benefit from the low cost and power offered by this much loved device.

Some commonly used terms

3G /4G internet – they refer to the third and fourth generation of mobile phone standards as set by the International Telecommunications Union (ITU). In theory, they are capable of much higher speed than standard broadband internet, with 4G being faster.

ATA - Analogue Telephone Adaptor - This is a small adaptor, usually about the size of a cigarette packet, which you plug into a normal phone to allow it to connect to a VoIP network and send calls over the Internet.

Bandwidth - Is the amount or volume of data that can be transmitted over an Internet or communication line in a given amount of time. It is measured in bits per second (bps) e.g., 10 mbps for Internet speed, and Hertz (Hz) for phone/analogue systems. The higher the number, the faster communication will be.

DHCP - Dynamic Host Configuration Protocol - DHCP is a protocol used by networked computers (clients) to obtain IP addresses and other parameters such as the default gateway, subnet mash, and IP addresses of DNS servers from a DHCP server. The DHCP server ensures that all IP addresses are unique.

DECT - Digital Enhanced Cordless Technology; they are basically wireless telephones that generally work with standard telephone lines (PSTN).

FXO - Foreign eXchange Office is a port that connects a device to a standard telephone line.

GSM - Global System for Mobile communication is a digital mobile telephony system that is widely used in Europe.

Internet Telephony – Making telephone calls over an internet connection.

IP Address - An IP address is a unique address that certain electronic devices use in order to identify and communicate with each other on a computer network utilising the Internet Protocol standard. Any participating network device can have its own unique address.

IVR - Interactive Voice Response - IVR or interactive voice response is a phone technology that allows a computer to detect voice and touch tones using a normal phone call. The IVR system can respond with pre-recorded or dynamically generated audio to further direct callers on how to proceed. IVR systems can be used to control almost any function where the interface can be broken down into a series of simple menu choices.

PBX - Private Branch Exchange - PBX stands for Private Branch eXchange which operates as a connection between a private organisation and the public switched telephone network (PSTN). It is a system which connects the outside telephone network to the internal telephones, fax machines and extensions within the business. Often a PBX will include features like speed dial, conference calling and music on hold.

PSTN - Public Switched Telephone Network - The public switched telephone network is the network of the world's public circuit switched telephone networks. Originally the PSTN was a network of analogue telephone systems but now the PSTN is entirely digital. The PSTN is largely governed by technical standards created by the ITU-T and uses E.163/E.164 address (commonly known as telephone numbers) for addressing.

Router - A router is a device that determines the proper path for data to travel between different networks and forwards data packets to the next device along this path. They connect networks together; a LAN to a WAN for example, to access the Internet. Routers are available in both wireless and wired versions.

SIP - Session Initiation Protocol is a protocol used in Voice over internet protocol communications allowing users to make voice and video calls.

SSID - service set identifier, name of a WIFI network.

VOIP – Voice over internet protocol is the technology of using the internet protocol for telecommunication, it is often confused with IP Telephony.

www.ingramcontent.com/pod-product-compliance
Lightning Source LLC
Chambersburg PA
CBHW072228170526
45158CB00002BA/803